START YOUR CAREER JOURNEY HERE!

Brian Mooney

The Educational Company of Ireland

Edco

First published 2014

The Educational Company of Ireland
Ballymount Road
Walkinstown
Dublin 12

www.edco.ie

A member of the Smurfit Kappa Group plc

ISBN: 978-1-84536-638-4
Book design: Liz White Designs
Cover design: Identikit
Layout: Outburst Design
Editor: Aoife Barrett
Proof-reader: Eleanor Ashe
Cover photography: iStockphoto.com

The paper used in this book comes from Managed Forests in Northern Europe For every tree felled, at least one new tree is planted

For permission to reproduce photographs, the author and publisher gratefully acknowledges the following: iStock.com; Shutterstock.com; Section 1 illustration © Tracy Brady; second image p. 4, *The Irish Times*/Institute of Guidance Counsellors RDS Higher Options Conference © *The Irish Times*; p. 13 National Framework of Qualifications © QQI 2014; The Script, pp. 28–29 © Peter Neill, ShootTheSound.com; p. 46 Danny Ryan © Ella Ryan; David Marshall images, p. 78 © Shane McCarthy Photography; pp. 101–104 © Irish Defence Forces.

Acknowledgements

The author and publisher would like to acknowledge the valuable assistance and expertise of the following people whose skills were invaluable in compiling the book:

Kara McGann, Policy Executive, Ibec (Irish Business and Employers Confederation); Captain Brendan O'Dowd, Air Corps Press Office, Irish Defence Forces; Dr Phillip Matthews, President of National College of Ireland; Dr John Mc Ginnity, Admissions Officer/Assistant Registrar NUI Maynooth; Deirdre Hanamy, Principal Blackrock Further Education Institute; Laura Nolan, Liaison Office Institute of Technology Tallaght; Kathy Murphy, University College Dublin.; Danny Ryan and Emily O'Reilly; Glen Power, The Script; David Marshall, David Marshall School of Hairdressing; Padraig Ó Cosgora, Trainee Manager, Lidl; Graham Doyle, Communications and Customer Service Manager, SUSI (Student Universal Support Ireland); Eileen Keleghan, Communications Officer, Central Applications Office; Ivor Gleeson, CEO, Central Applications Office; Susan MacNeill, Corporate Affairs and Communications, Quality and Qualifications Ireland; Noeleen Reade, Press Office, Department of Social Protection; Sarah Nash, Study Options ; Pippa Halley, Irish Program Manager, The Fulbright Commission/Education USA; James Durant, UCAS (Universities and Colleges Admissions Service); Guy Flouch, EUNiCAS (European Universities Central Application Support Service); Claire Looby, *The Irish Times*; Tom Farrell, Institute Guidance Counsellors; John Carton, Careers Portal; Eimear Sinnott, Careers Portal; Joanne Heffernan, Oatlands College; Kathleen Curtin, Oatlands College.

CONTENTS

Section Two

Your career journey will last a lifetime and will be influenced and directed by your innate abilities and the interests that you acquire. Given the dynamic nature of the world we live in, if you decide to study in college this year and then take a postgraduate programme to direct you into your first job, the world of work you encounter will probably be very different from today's labour market, so deciding what job you want to work in is not a major issue this year. All you have to figure out is the next appropriate step in your career journey. If you get this step right, the next one will fall into place in due course.

In *Start Your Career Journey Here!* you will find a road map to assist you as you set out on your lifelong voyage of discovery. It is laid out on a monthly basis, with all the important information you will need to engage with from this September until you receive your Leaving Certificate results next August. It also features reflections from people who are happy to share their career journey experiences with you.

The book contains a wealth of information including the best way to deal with the CAO application process, options for studying abroad, scholarships, apprenticeships, supports for those living with a disability, government employment schemes, taking a gap year and so on. There are also references throughout the book to useful websites, and advice on how to get the most out of them.

Writing this book over the past year has become a precious part of my own career journey. The encouragement and support of Martina Harford, CEO of the Educational Company of Ireland (Edco), who asked me to consider writing it, and of Aoife Barrett, Managing Editor of Barrett Editing, without whose wide range of personal and professional skills it could never have been written, have sustained me in bringing it to completion. My colleague Guidance Counsellor in Oatlands College, Tracy Brady, proved an invaluable source of professional support as I wrote it. Her drawing of the bird launching itself into flight on the following page perfectly encapsulates the theme and purpose of this book.

Some of the most creative ideas came from my wife and partner of forty years, Teresa, who has always been my most honest and caring critic.

I wish to dedicate this book to two women who have in their own way been central in shaping my life. Noreen Mooney, my beloved mother, and Johanna Leyden, my beloved mother-in-law, represent all that is best in Mná na hÉireann. Already in their tenth decade of life, may they both enjoy health and happiness for many years to come.

I hope that within its pages you will find the supports you need to successfully launch yourself into the adult world next August.

Brian

Leabharlanna Poiblí Chathair Baile Átha Cliath

Dublin City Public Libraries

Section 1

1 September

SEPTEMBER FOCUS

- Griffith Colleges in Limerick, Cork and Dublin, the Dublin Business School, Independent College Dublin, NUI Maynooth–Kilkenny and the National College of Ireland all hold Open Days throughout September.
- UCAS applications begin from mid-September and Open Days take place at the University of Ulster, Queen's University Belfast, University of South Wales and St Mary's University College London.
- Check out Beauty Academy Ltd., Pulse College, Irish College of Humanities & Applied Sciences, Dorset College, Open Training College, Bray Institute of Further Education, Portobello Institute, IT Blanchardstown, IT Cork, IT Tallaght and Galway-Mayo IT for September Open Days.
- NUI Galway and University College Cork, host a HPAT–Ireland information session for students interested in studying medicine.
- Registrations close towards the end of the month for the UKCAT if you want to apply for medical and dentistry schools in the UK.
- Career events in September include Career Zoo, Working Abroad Newcomers Network Dublin & Belfast and Which Course Expo.
- The *Irish Times*/Institute of Guidance Counsellors Higher Options Conference takes place in the RDS, Dublin.

Planning Your Exit from Second Level Education

Every September since you started school you have gone through the same routine – get out the uniform, organise your school books and sort out your alarm clock. This year you have just done this for the last time. In June next year, if everything goes according to plan, you will walk out of your school

following the completion of your Leaving Certificate and never return again as a pupil.

Between now and then you will have to make one very important decision – what am I going to do next? Many 6th Year students believe that when they answer this question they are deciding what occupation or career path they will follow for the rest of their working life. In fact none of us can ever make such a lifelong decision. All we can ever do is look at the evidence available to us today and then try to determine the next career step we want to take.

If you have arrived back at school this month with no particular idea about what you would like to do after you finish your Leaving Certificate in June next year you are not alone.

Tens of thousands of students are in a similar situation. No matter what others may expect of you, nothing is predetermined regarding your future when you are eighteen or nineteen years of age. The fact that you are doing your Leaving Certificate next June, and that you are leaving school behind you, does not mean that you have to decide your lifetime occupation right now. Developing your career plan is not a short-term project to be finalised over the next six to nine months. Instead your career strategy will grow and develop over the rest of your working life. The only question you need to concern yourself with in the short- to medium-term is: 'What is the first appropriate step on my lifelong career journey?'

As a guidance counsellor I am well used to having 6th Year students tell me that they have no idea what they want to do for the rest of their lives. My answer is that having worked for over forty years I'm still working that out for myself! All any of us can do is to look at our lives to date, explore all of the evidence which our life journey has provided, reflect on it and ask ourselves the questions below:

> What is the best thing I can do next year to advance my career prospects?
>
> Can I broaden the range of choices open to me or expand my options by the decisions I take over the coming months?

Any decision you take now can be reviewed by you as you proceed along your career pathway. We all make mistakes every day. What differentiates the most successful people in the world from everybody else is that they never see making a mistake as a failure. Instead they ask themselves: 'What have I learnt from this mistake?' Many venture capitalists will only ever

Top Tip!

Nothing is set in stone and if you find that you have made a choice that is not the correct one for you, just step back and reconsider your options.

consider investing in a business where the entrepreneur has had at least one, if not more, failed business projects behind them.

Learn from your previous mistakes and before you start into your final school year allocate time to seriously consider your career options. Accept that it is vitally important that you apply as much energy and thought into making the correct decision about your first career step, as you do into achieving the highest grades possible in your Leaving Certificate.

Points to note

Making mistakes, even though you may learn a lot from them, can be very expensive in the short-term. For example, deciding to drop out of a third level college course you select at the end of 6th Year to start into a new course the following academic year has serious financial consequences.

You may have to pay €3,000 registration charges if you start a course offered to you through the CAO application process next September.

The college will also receive for each student a minimum of €4,000–€5,000 from the Higher Education Authority (HEA) on behalf of the Department of Education and Skills (DES). The HEA rules state clearly that you can receive this payment only once for every year of your approved course.

If you change courses and repeat 1st year in college you will pay the full cost for that repeat year – a total of approx. €8,000. This rule applies even if you have paid for your own fees in a private college because such fees are deductible against your parents' tax bill at the standard rate.

So, review and carefully consider all your choices before you accept a place on a third level course.

Where Do I Start?

- There are a number of clues already in existence, within your life story, which will assist you in deciding what to do next. The trick is to link them all together to see if a pattern or picture emerges.
- Visit your guidance counsellor to help you look at the pattern of your life to date. This pattern is being woven daily through how you express yourself in all aspects of your life, including personal, educational, sporting, musical, social and vocational.
- Look at Section 2 of this book to find information on the many possible options open to you after the completion of your Leaving Certificate, e.g. studying abroad, PLCs, apprenticeships, employment and so on.
- Many of the career supports available are online, e.g. check out the websites www.careersportal.ie and www.qualifax.ie.

- Use this book as a reference point for your actions throughout the school year ahead. Read the relevant chapters as you proceed and always write down your reflections following any important career event, such as the Higher Options Conference, after a college Open Day or following a talk in school from an external speaker.

Higher Options Conference

Sixth Year starts for many of you with a visit to the *Irish Times*/Institute of Guidance Counsellors, three-day Higher Options Conference, in the RDS, Dublin. Over 25,000 Leaving Certificate students visit this exhibition each year. Hundreds of colleges in Ireland, plus numerous colleges from the UK, the continental EU, the USA and further afield, attend. Students can also talk to representatives from many other organisations and go to a series of

lectures on all aspects of college entry, including a detailed one from the CAO on the Irish third level application system. Similar exhibitions on a smaller scale are organised for students living outside Dublin by regional branches of the Institute of Guidance Counsellors throughout Ireland.

After your Leaving Certificate exams finish next June, you will have at least ten days to sit down and review everything you have researched, before you have to make any final decisions relating to your CAO college choices. If you use this book effectively you will have all of the information at hand to get that decision right when the day arrives.

The First Step

The key to making any important decision in life, particularly one that will shape your future, can be encapsulated in four simple words:

COME TO KNOW YOURSELF!

One of the most important lessons anyone can learn is that the answer to most of our important dilemmas lies within ourselves, if only we will take the time and effort to look.

External Sources of Information for Students

The Irish Universities Quality Board published a report on the type of information that prospective college students require. The report clearly outlines where prospective students are sourcing the relevant information on third level choices:

> 81% Use a range of websites.
>
> 79% Work with their guidance counsellor.
>
> 59% Attend Open Days.
>
> 39% Access information from friends.

Prospective students also:

- Visit colleges and talk to staff and students about their particular course and career aspirations.

- Read career literature and watch DVDs and online material published by colleges and professional bodies who represent particular careers.

The core of what you are asking yourself in this your final year as a second level student is: What kind of a person am I? What form of work will give me a strong sense of personal fulfilment and enrichment? This is not about how much you will earn in whatever job or occupation you eventually select either. Start on the journey of life with an open mind and be willing to consider all options open to you.

You were born with a unique basket of innate skills and talents; some of which you may not have even discovered as yet. You have been building on that base for eighteen years now and there is a huge reservoir of clues about where your career may be heading in the history of those years. So, look outwards, using all the sources of information available in this book to inform your future career choices, but always reflect on that data in the light of your own life journey to date. Your ultimate decision may be to apply for a college place next September or to volunteer to work for a charity abroad for a year or to do something completely different. The choice is yours and only you can ultimately know what is right for you.

Follow the Clues

If you were to sit down today and write out a list of everything you could possibly say about yourself, what would be on that list? Doing this is by far the best way to start figuring out the direction your life should take. We all have a wide range of interests, hobbies, skills, aptitudes and achievements, both academic and personal. The trick is to put them all together on a list, so that you can see if there is any pattern or recurring theme among them.

The list does not have to be structured. It can simply be a record of observations, key words, important highlights, happiest memories, your favourite things, hobbies or sports you enjoy participating in, anything that relates specifically to yourself.

Look at the sample questions below to help get you started with your list.

- What do you enjoy doing?
- Are you the outdoor type, who loves the freedom of being in the open air or are you more at home indoors, for example going to the cinema or cooking a gourmet feast?
- Are you good with people and do you enjoy helping or caring for them?
- Do you like making things or taking things apart to see how they work and then putting them back together?
- Are you artistic or musical or very involved in sports?
- Are you entrepreneurial, having bought and sold things among your friends and made a profit in the process?
- Have you been involved in a particular career through helping out at home in some aspect of a family business or profession. For example, the sons and daughters of politicians often also end up in politics because they have been dealing with people calling to their door day and night since they were young children. The life of politics becomes second nature to them.
- Do you like regular routine and enjoy organising your room so you can find anything at a moment's notice?
- What role do you play within your peer group? Are you the person with the ideas or the one who organises activities, or are you the peacemaker?

The answers to all of these questions will give you clues to your future career journey.

You should of course include your school life as well.

- What are your favourite subjects in school? Do you prefer languages, the sciences, business and technology subjects, the creative arts, music and so on?

Points to note

Aptitude tests are designed to discover your innate talents and skills through a series of timed tests. Abstract, Verbal, Numerical, and Spatial Reasoning are the four central competencies tested, and the questions within each aptitude become progressively more difficult so as to help identify those who are particularly skilled in one area. Other areas tested include Spelling, Arithmetic Calculation, Working Quickly and Accurately, Mechanical Reasoning and so on. The results are always presented to you and can be interpreted by a qualified guidance counsellor who will outline the implications of the test's findings in terms of the course or career options you are considering.

- What subjects have you always performed well in for school exams and in your Junior Certificate or GCSEs?

- What subjects did you select for your Leaving Certificate and why?

- You probably took a set of aptitude tests, either at the end of your Junior Certificate year or Transition Year. Did they indicate that you were strong in numerical, linguistic, abstract, mechanical, organisational reasoning or so on? If they did this is a particularly important clue in establishing your pattern of life to date.

- What have you enjoyed most in your years travelling up through primary and second level education? Was it particular subjects, teachers, activities or challenges?

- Were there subjects you would have liked to study but were unable to because they were not offered in your school or you had a clash of subject choices at the beginning of 5th Year?

- Have you taken any interest inventories in recent years to assist you in choosing your Leaving Certificate subjects? Did they indicate any particular career or course area that you had a stronger interest in than others?

- Genetics or family interests may also come into it. Is there any particular pattern within your own family that might give you a clue towards what direction your own career might take? For example, a proportion of your relatives may be teachers, electricians, Gardaí, retailers and so on.

Points to note

An Interest Inventory is a test designed around a series of questions that allow you to state your preference for one type of work over another. Interest inventories can be completed by you at no cost, on the Qualifax and Careers Portal websites. Many guidance counsellors also use Centigrade, an interest inventory provided by Cambridge Occupational Analysts that links your occupational interests with the entire database of courses on offer to you from all application systems.

When you have completed this exercise take out a highlighter and re-read what you have written, marking the words you feel are most significant.

Look at your list again to see if there is any pattern to it. In most cases, you may see a theme or possible area of interest emerging. This will inform your research in the months ahead.

From time to time over the next nine months take out this document and see if you can add anything new to it – anything that complements the picture of yourself to date.

Top Tip!

Of all of the sources of information that will enable you to come to a wise decision regarding your future next summer, this document will be by far the most important.

Tap into Your Parents' Expertise

From September onwards, your parents will want to help in whatever way they can as you work through the process of choosing a career. But they must realise that your career choice is just that – yours. Parents cannot live their lives through their children and cannot impose their own hopes and dreams on them. You must form your own dreams and your parents must learn to guide and assist you but not to dictate where you go after you leave school.

The world has changed enormously since your parents made their own career choice and it would be wrong for them to believe that they know best when it comes to deciding what career path you should follow. Do listen to your parents' advice, however, as they have huge wisdom based on having lived through many experiences. They may also be an invaluable source of information and support in teasing out where you want to start your career journey.

The most confused and bewildered students I've met are the ones attempting to live out their parents' expectations. The only thing worse is where two parents engage in power games through their child, with each parent attempting to get their son/daughter to pursue an unsuitable career aspiration that is their parents choice of occupation.

WAAAAHHH!!!

Parental advice is invaluable but you must make and own your particular career choices.

How to Use Your Guidance Counsellor

Career guidance at senior cycle level in second level schools covers three main areas:

✓ **Stimulating career development.**
✓ **Providing the forum for exploration and discussion.**
✓ **Aiding placement.**

Your Guidance Counsellor Helps You To:

1. Explore your attitudes to higher and further education, training and employment.

2. Manage your successful transition from post-primary school to further or higher education, training or employment.

3. Develop your use of research and ICT skills so that you can be self-directed in your career exploration and development.

4. Learn about job search and job retention skills, especially in the context of students taking the Leaving Certificate Applied and the Leaving Certificate Vocational Programme.

5. Understand the world of work, including employment rights and responsibilities.

6. Acquire and understand information about further and higher education and training courses, including course content, workload and progression routes.

7. Acquire and understand information prepared by public bodies, public agencies, and employers, regarding career opportunities they offer.

8. Contact and develop linkages with colleges of further and higher education and training organisations, to help you make your decisions regarding course and college choices.

9 Provides you with opportunities to attend events such as college open days, career fairs and visits by and to employers.

10 Comprehend the reality of working in particular careers, through presentations by past pupils and parents on their specific career area.

11 Differentiate between the career expectations you are beginning to develop for yourself as compared to the expectations that your parents may hold for you.

12 Identify careers that match those selected for you through psychometric instruments and other means of research and which are in line with your interests and aptitudes.

13 Obtain the skills to perform effectively in interviews through the organisation of mock interviews, usually with a panel of parents.

14 Understand the financial supports that may be available through the grants system to enable you to finance yourself through college.

Career Events

There are career events taking place every day of the year from the beginning of September right through to after the offers of CAO places in the middle of August next. If you were so foolish you could be out of school every day attending a career event in some college or other. With this in mind, it is vitally important that you sit down now and examine the full list of career events that are taking place during the coming school year and highlight the ones that you believe are relevant to your future career interests.

The biggest and most comprehensive career event is the Higher Options Conference, which takes place in September – see page 4. Many third level and further education colleges also visit schools to make presentations to 6th Year students between September and January each year, to highlight the benefits of attending their particular college or faculty. These visits are very professional, usually involving a 30-minute PowerPoint presentation. You will also attend Open Days laid on by the colleges for you during these months.

Points to note

A major concern of both guidance counsellors and school management is to ensure that these career-related activities do not interfere with your academic progression through 6th Year. For this reason, guidance counsellors usually facilitate your attendance at a restricted number of out-of-school events, so as not to disrupt your studies too much.

Top Tip!
You will find a full list of career events on the www.qualifax.ie website.

Getting the Most from a Career Event

If you do not sit down and plan what you want to find out from the stand-holders at career events you are wasting both your time and theirs.

You are also likely to make a total mess of making the successful transition from school to the world of further education, training or employment. Look at the Qualifiax website for worksheets to enable you to prepare for any career event you attend during the coming year. If you put in the effort now you won't waste your valuable time at the event and you will have a much more effective experience.

CAREER
☑ Advancement Potential
☑ Making a Difference
☑ Enjoyabl

Quality and Qualifications Ireland

Quality and Qualifications Ireland (QQI) was established in 2012. The new integrated agency replaces the Further Education and Training Awards Council (FETAC), the Higher Education and Training Awards Council (HETAC) and the National Qualifications Authority of Ireland (NQAI). It also incorporates the functions of the Irish Universities Quality Board.

QQI is responsible for the external quality assurance of further and higher education and training (including English language provision) and for the maintenance, development and review of the National Framework of Qualifications (NFQ).

National Framework of Qualifications

The National Framework of Qualifications (NFQ) works on a 10-level system, and each level is based on nationally agreed standards of knowledge, skills and competencies. It provides a way to compare qualifications and to ensure that they are quality-assured and recognised at home and abroad.

The NFQ also includes different categories or classes of award types. For more information see www.nfq.ie

Points to note

All awards previously issued as FETAC or HETAC are now Quality and Qualifications Ireland (QQI) awards. Students securing certification at Levels 1-6 of the National Framework of Qualifications (NFQ) for further education and training awards will receive a 'QQI Award–Further Education and Training Award' or a 'QQI Award–Higher Education and Training Award' for higher education and training qualifications at Levels 6-10 on the National Framework of Qualifications.

The State Examinations Commission (SEC) and Irish Universities and the Institutes of Technology will continue to make awards in their own right.

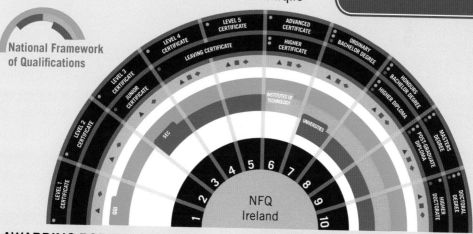

AWARDING BODIES

- Quality and Qualifications Ireland (QQI) makes awards in further and higher education and training
- SEC - State Examinations Commission (Department of Education and Skills)
- Institutes of Technology
- Universities

European Qualifications Framework

AWARDS IN THE FRAMEWORK

There are four classes of award in the National Framework of Qualifications:

- **Major Awards:** named in the outer rings, are the principal class of awards made at a level
- **Minor Awards:** are for partial completion of the outcomes for a Major Award
- **Supplemental Awards:** are for learning that is additional to a Major Award
- **Special Purpose Awards:** are for relatively narrow or purpose-specific achievement

For further Information consult: www.nfq.ie   www.QQI.ie

©QQI 2014

Looking at Options Abroad

If you are seriously considering studying outside of Ireland next year you may already be running up against application deadlines. For example, applications for the Universities and Colleges Admissions Service (UCAS) in the UK and Northern Ireland begin from mid-September. (See pages 40–45.) Many continental European Universities also have application dates early in the academic year. (See pages 54–56.)

Students who want to study in the United States need to start their research right away. In fact you should probably have started your research about six months ago, but September in 6th Year is not too late as long as you get moving right now! You need to select a range of colleges to approach and you have to book a place on the SAT (Scholastic Aptitude Testing) examination through the American Embassy. (See pages 165–169 for more information on studying in the United States of America.)

The same rules apply for those considering studies in Canada, Australia, New Zealand and so on. (See pages 169–173 for details about studying in Australia and New Zealand.)

EXTRA! EXTRA!

Do You Have an Exercise Plan to Help Manage Exam Stress?

So you have a study plan for your Leaving Certificate, but do you have a stress management plan? If not, here's something to consider.

A stressed brain = lower performance

When you become stressed and anxious, your body reacts by producing two key hormones – adrenaline and cortisol. Low levels of these two hormones can have a positive and performance enhancing effect; but high levels impair your brain's cognitive (thinking) ability and prolonged high levels can impair learning. So anything that helps you to manage stress more effectively will help to optimise your learning and consequently express more of your potential during the exams.

There are a number of ways to manage stress, including the reassurance that a well-thought out study plan gives, regular sleep, healthy diet and so on; but in addition to these, have you given any thought to the benefits of regular moderate exercise?

How Can Exercise Reduce Stress?

For many, the value of exercise in relieving stress may be perceived as having about as much benefit as a walk in the garden to 'clear the head'. But emerging research in the field of neuroscience is revealing that exercise may actually help to prevent the brain becoming stressed in the first place.

So here's the science:

The findings of a 2013 study at Princeton University by Timothy J. Schoenfeld, Pedro Rada, Pedro R. Pieruzzini, Brian Hsueh and Elizabeth Gould, were recently published in *The Journal of Neuroscience*.

From experiments conducted with mice, they found that 'regular physical activity reorganises the brain so that its response to stress is reduced and anxiety is less likely to interfere with normal brain function.' This ability of the brain to 'reorganise' itself is referred to by neuroscientists as neural plasticity.

The researchers reported that the brains of mice who exercised regularly 'exhibited a spike in the activity of neurons that shut off excitement in the ventral hippocampus, a brain region shown to regulate anxiety.' It appears that regular exercise causes changes in the brain that enable it to reduce stress and therefore to operate more effectively in a potentially stressful environment.

How Should I Incorporate Exercise into My Study Programme?

It may help to view your preparation for the Leaving Cert not as just a study programme, but as a holistic programme to ensure your optimal performance over the course of the exams. The study component of your preparation does not start in June of your final year (I hope!) so let's say it starts in September. Similarly the health and stress management components of your programme should start at the same time (if not before).

Given the emerging research discussed above, you should incorporate exercise into your weekly routine as soon as possible, so that you are 'training your brain'; encouraging those changes that will enable it to perform better when the stressful environment of June arrives. Just as with study, a good exercise plan will help you to establish a daily routine that (in time) becomes a habit and therefore easier to adhere to than to break.

How Hard and For How Long Should I Exercise?

There is an optimal intensity and duration for exercise that encourages a positive state in this context. You're not training for a marathon; you're exercising to encourage a healthy and resilient brain. Moderate exercise 30–35 minutes of every day, up to and including the two exam weeks, is both practical and optimal. What is moderate exercise for you will depend on your current fitness levels; but a decent yardstick is that you should be able to hold a conversation during the session and (over time) the fitter you get, the further you will be able to run, cycle, row, and so on in 30–35 minutes.

So consider the needs of your mind and your body; work these into your preparation and you will be preparing your brain for optimal performance throughout your study programme and through to the exams themselves. You'll also be adopting some great habits for the rest of your life!

Dr Phillip Matthews

President of National College of Ireland
(Former Ireland rugby captain)

2 October

- If you want to apply for a course in the UK or Northern Ireland the UCAS deadline for adding choices and accepting applicants is 15 October.
- Agricultural Colleges in Ballyhaise, Clonakilty, Gurteen, Kildalton and Mountbellew hold Open Days throughout the month.
- Universities including NUI Galway, University College Cork, University College Dublin, University of Limerick all host Information Evenings and Open Days in October.
- Career events this month include Career Options Cork, the National Careers Fair and Career Options West.
- Open Days at Institutes of Technology include Dundalk, Galway-Mayo, Limerick and Sligo.
- Check out Open Days at St Angela's College Sligo, College of Amenity Horticulture, the National Maritime College, Shannon College of Hotel Management and Mary Immaculate College.

After attending a major careers/colleges event, where you collected vast quantities of data on the opportunities available to you next year, you may be feeling like a rabbit in the headlights as you try to make sense of it all.

Your teachers are also constantly reminding you that throughout the remainder of this school year, every day and class counts in determining how well you are going to do in your Leaving Certificate. By now, if you are wise, you will have already put a study routine in place to ensure that you maximise your potential in June. But you should also have allotted some time to look at your future career plans.

Life after the Leaving Certificate

What have you done in the past month in preparation for the big decisions you will have to make as the school year draws to a close?

- Have you gone to a careers event either in your local area or to one of those organised at provincial or county level by the Institute of Guidance Counsellors?

- Have you attended or are you planning to attend any of the Open Days hosted by the universities and institutes of technology during October?

- Have any of the events you've already attended helped you to clarify your options for your life after 6th Year?

Digital Career Guidance Resources

Apart from attending career events outside of school there are a wide variety of sources of information and support available to you online. You should be utilising these websites on a regular basis as they will facilitate your decision-making process in determining what course of action to take next summer.

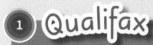

① Qualifax

www.qualifax.ie

The Qualifax website lists full details on every course offered in Ireland, many of which will be of interest to you as a 6th Year student, including:

- Post Leaving Certificate (PLC) courses – if you are considering one as a means of entering the labour market.
- Two-year Higher Certificate courses.
- Three-year Ordinary Degree or three/four year Higher Degree programmes, offered through the CAO.
- Postgraduate options which you may want to consider after you complete your initial undergraduate degree.

② Careers Portal

www.careersportal.ie

Careers Portal is a superb source of quality information on today's labour market and the world of employment. It will enable students exploring their options to see how the jobs that are available today relate to their own specific skills and interests. It was developed to complement the course information that is provided on Qualifax. With the rapid pace of technological change taking place in the economy today, the variety of post-school employment opportunities on offer has never been more diverse.

Hundreds of schools have registered with the 'Reach Programme' on the Careers Portal website and you would normally have registered as a user in Transition Year. If you don't already have an account, register now. You will have access to an entire programme of Apps which you can use to assist you in coming to a decision on the best course of action to take next year. Your research can then be stored in your careers portal account.

Even if your school is not a registered 'Reach' user, you can still access many of the resources on their website. The only difference is that your Guidance Counsellor will not be able to review your work. (See pages 24–27 for more information on how to use Careers Portal.)

③ UCAS

www.ucas.com

UCAS (Universities and Colleges Admissions Service) processes applications to third level institutes in Great Britain and Northern Ireland for both undergraduate and postgraduate courses. It is the equivalent of Ireland's CAO system. (See pages 40–45 for more information about their services.)

Top Tip!
If you want to apply for a place in professional medicine, dentistry, veterinary medicine or veterinary science courses, and for all courses offered by the university of Oxford or Cambridge, you have to submit your UCAS application online by midnight on 15 October, with a reference from a teacher, adviser or professional who knows you.

✓ If you are considering applying for any course offered through UCAS you can register your interest on its website from mid-September until 15 January next year.

✓ If you are interested in applying for medicine in the UK you have to register for a HPAT equivalent test. The two testing bodies involved in the UK are the British Medical Aptitude Test (BMAT) or the UK Clinical Aptitude Test (UKCAT).

✓ Even though several thousand Irish students seek medical places in UK universities each year, only a handful of applicants are successful. In 2013, twenty-five applicants in the Republic of Ireland secured a pre-clinical medical place in a UK University through UCAS.

④ EUNiCAS

www.eunicas.ie

EUNiCAS stands for European University Central Application Support Service. The website provides information on courses taught in Continental European Universities exclusively through the English language.

✓ Irish citizens are entitled to attend any courses in a publically-funded EU university on the same terms and condition as citizens of the country in question. In most cases, this is either on a no fees basis or on paying a fee that is significantly less than the €3,000 registration charge you will face in an Irish university.

✓ Another plus for Irish students is the entry requirements. Unlike in Ireland, where CAO points over and above matriculation are standard requirements, many European universities admit students if they meet the published entry requirements. Once you meet the matriculation grades (two higher level Cs and four Ds) you are likely to secure your place. Certain faculties do require higher grades, but the course requirements are usually still far lower than their CAO equivalent.

✓ Getting into your desired course may be far easier in some European universities than through the CAO system, but academic standards are still quite high. If you decide to study abroad you need to commit to your studies 100 per cent as otherwise you are likely to find yourself back home at the end of your First Year exams.

5 Central Applications Office (CAO)

www.cao.ie

Your Guidance Counsellor will have given you a copy of this year's CAO handbook by now. All of your communications with the office will be through their website. The CAO is like 'Grand Central Station' but instead of platforms and trains it facilitates getting you to the correct college and onto the right course!

You can register your interest with the CAO by signing up with it in the first week of November and creating your own password-protected account. Through links on its website you can explore any course, the Higher Education Access Route (HEAR) and Disability Access Route to Education (DARE) schemes, the Health Professions Admission Test (HPAT) application process for undergraduate medical places and many other options.

Top-Tip!

By 1 July next year, you will have to submit your final course preferences 1–10, using your CAO account. Your points score in the Leaving Certificate next August will determine which course you are offered.

6 Course Hub

www.coursehub.ie

The Course Hub website contains thousands of reviews of both colleges and individual courses written by current and past students. When you are beginning to seriously consider listing a particular course on your CAO application read the reviews written by students who have already taken the programme.

It will be extremely informative but it is no substitute for a personal visit. Try to go and see the colleges/individual faculties you are considering.

www.careersnews.ie

The former national director of Qualifax, Tom Farrell, has created a careers news website that contains the latest news items on all areas of career selection.

Many students register with the site in 6th Year as it is totally free and you will get a daily feed of news items, so nothing of importance will slip by you!

Exploring Courses Online

The Irish Universities Quality Board has published a report that shows which websites prospective students use most to explore course options:

84% www.qualifax.ie
55% www.careersportal.ie
49% www.cao.ie
25% A range of University and Institute of Technology websites

Point to note

The www.qualifiax.ie website allows you to tailor your search for courses by using the advanced search facility – filtering by keywords, counties, points, levels and so on.

When asked which websites they found most useful prospective students indicated the following levels of satisfaction with the most commonly used sites:

Qualifax 69%
Careers Portal 39%
CAO 31%
University Website 28%

Students were then asked what information they wanted to find out about when deciding to study a course at a particular college.

The top five ranking answers were as follows:

1. Course content and information about the course.

2. The quality of the degree/qualification.

3. The typical careers/jobs associated with the course.

4. What the learning outcomes will be from the course.

5. How much direct contact there will be with academic staff members.

Using the Websites Effectively

It is clear from the report that there is a wide range of sources of information available, from dedicated websites such as qualifax.ie and guidance counsellors in schools, to college open days as well as friends and family. The websites used by those researching their career options have various strengths:

- Qualifax is by far the most popular website for course content.
- The Careers Portal website covers the world of work.
- The CAO website is the ultimate source of accurate information on what courses are on offer from all colleges in the system and on the rules relating to applying for such courses.
- The universities own websites help students to get an insight into what attending a particular course will involve.

The five top questions on the minds of prospective students identified by the report will also help to guide you as you continue to research your options.

If you combine all this information with the career journey list you've been building since September, the chances are that you will choose the correct career path for yourself, when you have to make up your mind in the months ahead.

Top Tip! When you have narrowed down your choices to a small number of areas you should research every single course available in Ireland on www.qualifax.ie and the courses on offer abroad on www.eunicas.ie.

How to Use Careers Portal

To make the most of Careers Portal you should sign up and create your own Career File. This will give you access to the career exercises and enables you to store your career research online. It will also allow you to make shortlists of courses or occupations that interest you.

REACH+: Many students use the REACH+ Career and College Preparation Programme. This involves you and your guidance counsellor but most of the work can be undertaken independently by you.

Organising your Research Using the Career File

The Career File stores the results of the Interest and Personality Profiler tests, saves lists of courses and occupations of interest, and can store anything you come across that might be useful. REACH+ users have access to a more comprehensive Career File that includes over forty Apps and the ability to create a full Career Portfolio.

How to Create a Career File

Your Career File is created automatically once you register with Careers Portal. Choose the Sign Up button at the top left of any page and complete the simple registration form. It gives you access to:

Top Tip!
The results of these profilers are saved in your Career File for future reference.

- **Interest Profiler** – helps you find a general career direction.
- **Personality Profiler** – aims to identify your temperament and then suggests some typical characteristics and careers that 'fit' your personality.
- **Career Notepad** – an online word processor that can store anything you write into it. It is used for to-do lists, writing a CV, storing course/career details and so on. It contains a Toolbox that gives you access to the main search areas you are likely to need – courses, occupations and career sectors.

1 Discover Your Preferred Career Sectors

Careers Portal breaks the world of work into over thirty career sectors and provides a wealth of information on each one. Select the Sectors link on the main menu. If you have an interest in a particular sector, you will find lists of courses, sample occupations and career and course videos. Scan through these sectors and identify those that interest you. Become familiar with the different career opportunities and ask yourself some questions:

✓ Is this sector involved in something I am interested in?

✓ Are there any particular jobs that I could see myself in?

✓ If I was trained, would I be able to enjoy working in this area?

REACH+: You can use the Career Sectors App in your Career File to read through a quick summary of each sector. Select the sectors that interest you, giving them a score and they will be listed in your Favourites.

2 Discover your Career Interests – Interest Profiler

Follow the link to the Interest Profiler. The questions should take 10–20 minutes and produce a graphical representation of your interests.

- You will be presented with a three-letter code indicating your three highest scoring interest categories.
- Read the quick descriptions and decide for yourself which three interests are your strongest and in which order.
- These codes are then used to suggest careers that may interest you. You can cross-check them against hundreds of careers and courses you may be considering, to see how they match your interests.

REACH+: You can write up a summary report on your interests online, identifying which interests describe you the best and why.

Using the Results

Explore Careers link – to get a listing of occupations that match your career interests. You can apply filters to narrow down the results to restrict them to career sectors that interest you. Up to four can be selected at any one time.

Explore CAO/QQI (formerly HETAC and FETAC)/PLC Courses – follow the Explore CAO/PLC links to use your interests to help find courses that may suit you. Use the filters on the search page to narrow down the list of courses. Your objective is to form a shortlist. They are ranked alphabetically. If a course looks interesting, click the 'add' button to save it to your favourites.

3 Exploring Careers

Careers Portal has information on 900 occupations, with videos and career interviews from Irish workers. Over 1,500 additional links to online videos (YouTube etc.) and resources are integrated into the database, and it is continuously being updated. View as much video material as you can and ask yourself the following questions:

✓ Can you see yourself in that role?

✓ Is there a good fit between the work and your career interests/personality?

✓ Is the typical pay acceptable?

✓ What qualifications would you need and are their courses available?

The Occupation pages list related courses from both PLC/QQI (formerly FETAC) and CAO/ QQI (formerly HETAC) course databases. Additionally, there is a link to Qualifax and their database of courses related to the occupation.

4 Exploring Courses

Unique tools will help you search for courses in Ireland. The CAO and PLC Wizards take you step-by-step through a number of choices to produce a list of courses that match your requirements.

- **Simple Search** – for a quick look at courses by title, code, sector or college.
- **STEM Courses** – for courses related to Science, Technology, Engineering and Mathematics.
- **Restricted Courses** – lists all courses that require a portfolio or interview as part of the application process.
- **New Courses** – lists all courses that are new for the next application period.

Top Tip!

A Guidance Toolbox helps you with your research – including a Points Calculator, Course Investigation Worksheet and a CAO Guide.

Choosing CAO Courses – the CAO Wizard

The CAO Wizard contains six steps that enable you to select courses that interest you. If you have completed the Interest Profiler, you can access the Wizard from your results page. You can choose filters including:

- Level 6/7 courses and/or Level 8 courses – handy for making lists for your CAO application.
- Courses up to a certain points score.
- Courses based on your Leaving Certificate subjects.
- Direct Entry courses – these are mostly run by fee-paying, private colleges and applications are made directly to the college.

Exploring Individual Courses

Careers Portal provides:

- A **brief description** of courses, careers and further education opportunities.
- Links to the **detailed course information** from the college and from Qualifax.
- **Related course suggestions** – lists similar courses from colleges in the same region.
- **News and Events** directly from the college.
- **CAO points** – a comparison with the previous year's and a historical list of points so you can see the trends.
- **Course videos**, giving a good insight into what the course has to offer.
- **Career Interviews** from people who have already taken the course.

Choosing PLC Courses – the PLC Wizard

The PLC Wizard provides the same services as detailed in the Exploring Individual Courses section above and it also features:

QQI (formerly FETAC) progression routes, where available. You can get a list of all CAO courses where the QQI course award is accepted as an entry option.

REACH+ Users: within the PLC Choices App use the Find Courses link. You will be able to access a version of the PLC Wizard search that also includes your career interests if you have completed the Interest Profiler. The **Evaluate Courses Section** will list all your course favourites and a checklist of factors that you may find important for choosing a college and course. You can score the content of each course, and how it matches up to the factors you consider important. Links are provided to course details, and you can write comments in terms of what you like/ dislike most. You can then rank your list in order of preference and save it.

5 Keep Informed – News/Facebook/Twitter

www.facebook.com/CareersPortal   www.twitter.com/CareersPortal

Keep in touch with important career news on the home page and watch out for the notices and events posted on the Colleges Direct areas of the site.

REACH+: In your Career File you will have a Guidance noticeboard near the top right of your screen. This always contains a direct link to the Qualifax Events Calendar – listing just about every event that relates to career guidance in the country. In both the **Open Days** and **Careers Fairs** Apps you can view a list of upcoming events throughout Ireland.

Careers Portal has Facebook and Twitter pages that are continually updated with career and jobs news relevant to students. Follow them for alerts on the many jobs, courses or training options that become available.

I Want To Be a Musician

I was asked to write a bit about my experience with school, academics and life after school. To be honest about it, I was not a very academic pupil. To be fair, I was a bit of an entertainer and joked around quite a bit, so I'm sure that didn't help!

But I was very lucky early on to find that I had a talent for music. Music was a big thing in my house. My Dad is a singer, so it was constantly around.

I think the biggest success in life is finding what you are good at, naturally good at, and what you Love to do. Each of us is unique and we all have something to give to the world. The saddest thing in life is to find out what that is and to not use it or to not be encouraged by those around you to nurture and bring forth that talent in every way possible.

Sometimes the facilities are simply not there, which is just down to the environment you're in and the tools that people have to work with. Unfortunately for me, Music was not catered for when I was in school. It was not on the Curriculum.

So I had to get lessons privately, outside of school hours. What I realised very quickly was that I had natural rhythm. It came easy to me. I learned this from the group classes I took as I worked my way from Intermediate to Advanced Class very quickly.

I knew somewhere deep down inside my core that this was the path for me – Music, all the way, no matter what. It made me feel connected, alive and grounded. There was never any doubt when it came to music for me,

I **KNEW** it was the right thing for me to be doing and as a young kid it was probably the only thing I was sure of!

I fondly remember the day when in 3rd year I had a meeting with my Career Guidance teacher to talk about my future Goals/Aspirations and choice of Career.

'I want to do Music. I want to be a Musician,' I said.

'That's fine as a hobby, but what about a career?' he replied.

'That's what I mean. I want to do Music as a career. I want THAT to be my full-time job.'

'You need something to fall back on; you need a career, something ACADEMIC.'

'I'll fall back on Music, that's what I want to do. Why can't I do that? Look at U2 – they're Irish, they have two arms and two legs. I'm the same. I'm Irish; why can't I do that?'

'Well that's U2; they're different. That's a whole different thing!'

Long story short, I disagreed with him.

But what if I didn't? What if I had listened?

Would I be sitting here right now in America, in The Script, on tour with the band I'm in? Waiting to go onstage tonight to play for 20,000 people?

With sales of over 20 million records worldwide?

No, I wouldn't.

I would more than likely be sitting back in Dublin, doing something I don't love, with the dream of being a Musician long forgotten. Life would have well and truly taken over and that dream would be fading and fading, with each passing year reinforcing the belief that it was never possible. But, I believed and went for it.

Not that this whole journey was by any means easy. I'm playing music now over twenty-four years professionally and it's really only in the last eight years that things really took off in a big way for me. But I was always playing, always hustling, always working.

I **NEVER** gave up on the dream I had as a kid when I was thirteen practising in my bedroom, dreaming of being up in front of massive crowds and feeling that feeling for real, the shivers rising and falling, up and down my spine as I imagined being up there onstage. I believe that the mere stirring up of that feeling in you vibrates you like a magnet and that 'like attracts like'.

I now do this every night **FOR REAL** all over the world. I'm living proof that if you have a dream and have a knowing in your heart that you want to do something, if you put in the hours, if you never give up and if you work hard enough for it – it **WILL HAPPEN**.

So for anyone reading this that feels like they are an outsider, feels like they don't fit in, are afraid to step-up and say 'I want to do this' and are afraid of the repercussions, I say:

Don't ever be afraid to be WHO YOU ARE,

Be more afraid of being WHO YOU ARE NOT,

Because in the long run, and as the years go by,

WHO YOU ARE will never be happy with

WHO YOU ARE NOT.

If you've been given Talents/Gifts, and you feel a pull in your heart and soul to nurture, grow and chase after them, follow your Heart and follow your Dream.

There is a reason you feel the way you do; it is real.

All you need to do is do the next right thing and I believe with faith, hard work and time, the Universe will answer.

If it did for me, it can and will for you.

Glen
The Script

3 November

NOVEMBER FOCUS

- CAO online applications can be made from early November on www.cao.ie
- Many of the Institute of Technology colleges hold Open Days in November. Check out the websites for dates in Athlone, Carlow, Cork, Dundalk, Galway-Mayo, Letterkenny, Limerick, Tallaght and Tralee.
- If you are focusing on studying in the USA, the SAT (Scholastic Aptitude Testing) examinations are run in various centres around Ireland throughout November.
- For students interested in studying or working in the UK, the Career Development Institute host a two-day Annual Conference and Exhibition.
  - The University College Dublin (UCD) Open Day and the Medicine visiting programme take place in November.
  - Dublin City University (DCU), NUI Galway, National College of Ireland and NUI Maynooth & Pontifical all run Open Days this month.
  - Mater Dei Institute of Education, Mary Immaculate Limerick, St Patrick's College Dublin, Marino Institute of Education and the Dun Laoghaire Institute of Art, Design & Technology, all hold Open Days in November.

Top Tip!

Don't forget to tick the SUSI box on your CAO application form if you intend applying for student funding. (See pages 119–122.)

The first week of November marks the beginning of the second half of the first term. It is a good time to review your progress. By now you may have:

✓ Identified a number of courses or possible career options which you are seriously considering.

✓ Attended a number of career events.

✓ Explored one or more of the career website listed in the previous section.

✓ Spoken at length with your guidance counsellor, if your school still has one.

✓ Added to the personal profile/history that you started writing in September.

Look-up entry requirements for architecture!

From all of this you may be beginning to identify a particular area of interest which will determine the choices you make next August. If that is as far as you can now see you are doing great.

Many 6th Years only begin to finally identify the options that they want to pursue in the last ten days of June, after they have completed the final written paper in their Leaving Certificate. That is why the CAO gives you until 5.15 p.m. on 1 July each year to make your final course choices.

The Central Admissions Office (CAO) Application Process

By now you should have a copy of the CAO Handbook – either from your guidance counsellor or by requesting one from its website.

Reading the CAO Handbook

It may seem like a statement of the obvious but you need to read the rules and regulations section carefully. Look at some of the other points you need to consider below:

- You can make an application to the CAO from 5 November up until 1 May next.
- When you apply to the CAO you are entering into a legal contract with them. The terms and conditions of the contract are set out in the front section of your handbook and they will not change, no matter what the circumstances. Guidance counsellors are sometimes lobbied by Government Ministers on behalf of students who made some mistake or other in the application process, asking that the error be overlooked and a place be offered to a constituent. The answer is always no.

- Avoid mistakes: the rules cannot be interfered with because your mistake has opened up a college place for another applicant who has met the terms of the contract. That applicant could sue the CAO if they were denied the place which was rightfully theirs, even if they only got the offer because of your mistake.

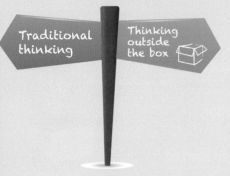

- As a 6th Year student in school it may be hard for you to accept that you have to live with the consequences if you make a serious mistake in your CAO college application. Why is this? Maybe because since you entered school as a five-year-old, adults have usually found ways to overcome the consequences of your mistakes. Coming to terms with these hard realities of life is in essence what growing up is about. Now that you are entering the adult world, you can no longer expect others to unravel the consequences of your actions or inactions, such as making a major error in completing your CAO application. You have to find solutions to the problems you create for yourself.

- So put some serious time aside in the next few days to read the terms and conditions of the contract the CAO is offering you in return for your €25 payment. You will benefit hugely from doing so.

- The second section of your CAO handbook contains the full list of all courses offered by the colleges who signed up to the CAO rule book when the handbook went to print last June. Since then the academic councils of many colleges have amended a number of courses on offer, withdrawn some existing programmes and approved new offerings. You need to check the amended courses list on www.cao.ie. It should always be read in conjunction with the list of courses on offer.

Top Tip!

The www. qualifax.ie website normally lists any course changes within 24-hours of notification by third level colleges, so you can trust a search of their database to give you the full list of courses on offer.

Restricted Courses

Before you put your CAO handbook aside for a while conduct one simple exercise.

1 Go through every course page and circle any option listed as restricted. The restricted identity tag will be on the right-hand side of the page, beside the course code and title which is on the left-hand side.

2 Now go back through the full list of restricted courses and ask yourself one simple question: Is there any way that I may be interested in studying any of these courses next year?

3 If you are even mildly interested in any of these courses you need to be aware of two things:

(i) You only have until 1 February next to list this course on your CAO application. If you discover after 1 February that you want to add a restricted course, you can amend your application list to add this course by paying the CAO an additional fee of €10 up until 1 March.

(ii) There is always some form of portfolio requirement, interview or performance aspect to a restricted course. You need to be clear about what that involves for your particular course so that you are fully prepared to present or perform on the required date. If the requirements are far more than you can manage while preparing for the exams you could concentrate on your Leaving Certificate subjects for now and identify a portfolio or performance preparation course which you can take as a Post Leaving Certificate (PLC) course in the coming academic year.

Top Tip!
All PLC courses are filled on a first come first served basis, following an interview. Check out the PLC colleges in your locality this month to see if they have any programmes you may wish to apply for.

PLC Courses

Post Leaving Certificate courses are not just useful for those looking to do portfolio preparations programmes. They also offer a wide variety of opportunities for students who have a particular talent in one specific area but may not do well across a seven subject Leaving Certificate.

Example: To secure a place on a science degree course in UCD you have to get up to 515 CAO points. But if you excel in a PLC science programme, and do very well across all eight modules of the course, you will have a strong chance of been offered a place in 1st Year Science in UCD at the end of your one year course. The same applies across a wide range of CAO courses.

If you want to explore this option further there is an extremely good module on the www.careersportal.ie website which shows the link between PLC programmes and CAO courses that offer reserved places to students on those courses. As yet, there is no centralised PLC application process, so each college accepts applications either on the printed application form provided at careers fairs or online on the individual college's websites. (See pages 141–143 for more information.)

EXTRA! EXTRA!

Getting that College Place

Ten recommended steps for you to make which will result in a successful college transition.

1 Get the balance right between your senior cycle studies for your exams and the 'extra subject' which is your career and college decision for life after school. The two are intertwined and ideally you want them working in harmony for you.

Your mantra should be that 'the three most important things in making the right career choice are research, research and research!'

2 Engage with your guidance counsellor during class periods and also in one-to-one meetings as you plan your choices. Your guidance counsellor will be able to work with you to identify possible career areas that would suit you based on their knowledge of your academic progress in the school and the feedback from psychometric and other tests that you may have undertaken.

3 Understand that any decision you make needs to be an informed one. Never before has there been so much information available, and so easily accessible. Each third level institution makes the course structure for each year of study, as well as all the electives, available online. Important information such as how each subject will be taught and the assessment methodology will provide you with insights as to how your knowledge in the college will be developed.

Key areas such as international study abroad, work placement, as well as career and postgraduate options may also be outlined. This college information can be used in tandem with valuable information which may be accessed on Qualifax. ie and Careersportal.ie.

4 Get the most out of career exhibitions you attend – don't be put off by what may seem a crowded area. Take time to speak to college advisors. They naturally want to help students just like you so don't be afraid to ask direct questions to help your decision making. They will have in-depth knowledge on all the programmes on offer and also choices that emerge at the end of first year, second year etc. – so get that insider knowledge!

⑤ Visit campuses both on structured Open Days and on other days when it is not an Open Day but rather a typical student day on campus. There will be days when your school is not in play yet the college is in session – so you will get a good sense of student life on campus. Drop into the Admissions team to have a chat about possible options that you may have interest in.

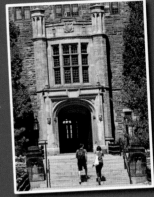

Be discerning when you go to an Open Day; plan your daily schedule in advance to make best use of your time. Avoid just following the crowds. Seek out students who are studying the course(s) you are considering to find out their experiences and also academics who teach on the programme (invariably they will inspire you as they are passionate about their own subject area). The aggregate of the information imparted to you from both academic staff and students will give you a comprehensive picture.

⑥ Watch out for summer schools or other focused days on campus that will allow you get a chance to spend some targeted time taking a deeper look at a particular subject area. Often a summer school will allow you to spend a day or a week exploring potential career interests and you will have a chance to see the facilities that the college has on offer.

⑦ Use family and friend networks to explore career areas – they will have important insights to share with you from their own experiences.

Be conscious of their biases – in the end it is *your* decision and it will be more valued if the career and college choice is one that you have made yourself for yourself, rather than a decision made for you by others.

⑧ Be strategic – apply for courses in the subject areas that you are interested in across a range of colleges, levels in the CAO and also in Colleges of Further Education. There are well worn pathways now with linkages across colleges and courses for a diverse range of students, with a range of different backgrounds. It is important to note, however, that transfer between colleges will depend on the grades you attained in your studies – these will be assessed by the college you wish to transfer to.

⑨ Don't try to be too clever about estimating CAO points! Simply place your CAO choices in your genuine order of preference and avoid the annual mistake made by thousands of students who try to second guess the points system only to their regret.

⑩ Remember – it is okay not to know what you wish to do after second level. However, it is important that you move through that state of mind towards getting to make the right decisions based on your mantra of research, research, research!

Best of luck in your decisions!

Dr John McGinnity
Admissions Officer/Assistant Registrar *NUI Maynooth*

4 December

- Check out the Open Day dates for Trinity College Dublin, Waterford IT, Limerick IT and Dublin IT, as they are usually the last major ones before the Christmas break.
- The National College of Art and Design Open Day and the Better Options College Fair at the National College of Ireland might also be of interest to you.
- SAT examinations are run in various centres around Ireland throughout December as well.
- The Church of Ireland College of Education run an Open Day for perspective B. Ed. Students in December as do the Pallaskenry Agricultural College, County Limerick.

EDUCATION MOTIVATION INSPIRATION CREATIVITY PARTNERSHIP ACCURACY

You are almost half way through sixth year now and your Christmas exams are imminent. From a careers perspective most of the main Irish college Open Days have taken place. It is now time to take stock and review the progress which you have made in clarifying your post-Leaving Certificate goals.

Completing the Initial CAO Registration Process

If you intend to apply for a third level place in the coming academic year through the CAO, you should by now have:

✓ Filled in the first section of the application process.

✓ Paid your €25 applications fee.

✓ Got your CAO application number.

- ✓ Indicated which school or schools you have attended during your second level education.

- ✓ You should also have read the rules and regulations surrounding the Disability Access Route to Education (DARE) and Higher Education Access Route (HEAR) schemes, details of which are outlined in the General Information section of the CAO handbook. Application guides are available at www.accesscollege.ie. It is essential to apply early as the applications can take some time to be processed. Clinics take place in January each year to answer any questions that prospective applicants and their parents might have.

What is HEAR?

The Higher Education Access Route (HEAR) is a college and university admissions scheme that offers places on reduced points and with extra college support to school leavers from socio-economically disadvantaged backgrounds. HEAR applicants must meet a range of financial, social and cultural indicators to be considered, e.g. be under twenty-three years of age and have completed the Leaving Certificate.

What is DARE?

The Disability Access Route to Education (DARE) is a third level admissions scheme that offers places on a reduced points basis to school leavers under twenty-three years of age with disabilities who have completed an Irish Leaving Certificate. DARE is for school-leavers who have the ability to succeed in higher education but who may not be able to meet the points for their preferred course due to the impact of their disability.interview or performance aspect to a restricted course. You need to be clear about what that involves for your particular course so that you are fully prepared to present or perform on the required date. If the requirements are far more than you can manage while preparing for the exams you could concentrate on your Leaving Certificate subjects for now and identify a portfolio or performance preparation course that you can take as a Post Leaving Certificate (PLC) course in the coming academic year.

Key-points!

How Do You Apply?

- Candidates must notify the CAO that they wish to apply to DARE and HEAR by 1 February.

- The HEAR application forms and the DARE Supplementary Information Form must be submitted to the CAO by the deadline of 1 March.

- By 1 April, DARE applicants must send evidence of their disability to the CAO (See www.accesscollege.ie/dare/evidence-disability.php) and a completed, signed and stamped Second Level Academic Reference downloadable from www.accesscollege.ie/dare/downloads.php.

- HEAR applicants must submit supporting documents to the CAO by 1 April. See the Application Checklist on www.cao.ie.

- DARE and HEAR applicants will receive a letter after the Leaving Certificate has finished in June, notifying them of whether or not they are eligible for the programmes. Course offers are issued as part of CAO Round 1.

Points to note

If you are applying for DARE because you have a diagnosis of one of the disabilities listed under the scheme, you need to secure a relevant consultant's report prior to the final date for submission of all documentation which is 1 April. If you have to get a consultant's appointment through the public health system, you must do this in December or you may end up missing the deadline.

Benefits of HEAR and DARE

What are the benefits of being classified under either scheme?

1. Both HEAR and DARE schemes allocate up to 5 per cent of the overall number of places available on each course in the participating institutions. The schemes offer courses in the universities, teacher training colleges and some of the institutes of technology. If you end up being accepted into HEAR or DARE, or both, you will be competing for one of these places and you will only be in competition with the other DARE or HEAR students who qualify.

2. The entry points required for HEAR and DARE places will be at least 10 per cent less, if not more in some cases, than the points necessary for the final student to be offered a place on the mainstream CAO entry list.

Studying in the UK or Northern Ireland

Each year 5,000–6,000 Leaving Certificate students try to secure places in universities in the UK and Northern Ireland through UCAS, the Universities and Colleges Admissions Service. You will find details on around 100,000 undergraduate and postgraduate courses, in a wide range of subjects on its website, www.ucas.com.

The courses have different application deadlines and entry requirements, so do plenty of research before you choose your subject and course provider. You can find advice on how to fill in your UCAS application in the undergraduate, performing arts, postgraduate and teacher training parts of the website.

Tuition Fees

- The numbers of Irish students who take up places has dropped in recent years following the introduction of fees of Stg£9,000 in English universities. These fees are not usually off-putting for students who are capable of securing an offer of a place in one of the highly prestigious world universities, such as Oxford or Cambridge, but they do give other students pause. However, whatever type of course it is – whether academic, performing arts or teaching training – these are the maximum tuition fees you have to pay each year. Some course providers charge less but many charge the full amount. Examine the course provider websites for details.

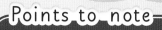

- Successful applicants to universities in Northern Ireland and Wales pay tuition fees of between Stg£3,575 and Stg£4,000.

- Through an anomaly in the system, Irish students studying in Scottish universities pay no fees, which results in about 400 students accepting places in Scotland each year, a similar number to those accepting places in Northern Ireland. Over 1,000 other students accept places in England and Wales.

- Four hundred and eighty (23%) of all successful Irish applicants secured places in nursing, with the top ten providers listed below, in ranked order:

Points to note

In 2013/14, UCAS recorded 6,056 applicants from the Republic of Ireland and 2,119 (35%) of them secured places. Of the successful candidates 1,365 were under 20 years of age, with 754 being aged 21 and over. The male/female breakdown was 711/1,408.

	Course Provider
1	Buckinghamshire New University
2	Edinburgh Napier University
3	Canterbury Christ Church University
4	The University of West London
5	University of Ulster
6	Middlesex University
7	Robert Gordon University
8	The University of Stirling
9	Kingston University
10	Queen's University Belfast

- Although only twenty-five students secured a pre-medical place in 2013, over 400 successful applicants secured places in the medical field, in areas such as anatomy, physiology, pathology, pharmacology, toxicology, pharmacy, medical technology and other subjects allied to medicine.

Financial Support

- As an EU applicant you may be eligible to apply for financial help with your undergraduate tuition fees and living costs. Check the student finance website for the UK region you want to study in to see if you qualify for funding.

- Some of the performance-based music, dance and drama courses may consider waiving the fee if you cannot afford to pay it and you have a successful performing arts audition.

- You may also be able to access student loans to pay fees in the UK. Repayments usually kick in a number of years after graduation, once your income has reached a certain level.

Top Tip!

If you qualify for a student grant in Ireland you can take it with you to a UK University or to a publically-funded EU university.

How Does the UCAS Application System Work?

The UCAS application process is completely different from the CAO process. Have a look at the various stages outlined below:

1 You register to use Apply and login to supply your personal details.

2 You may select up to five separate courses, all of which are of equal weight, i.e. you don't list them in order of preference. Make sure you have checked the entry requirements first.

Top Tip!

Every college in the UK is called a university no matter how humble its original background, so do your research well before you apply.

There are some restrictions. For example you can only have a maximum of four courses in any one of medicine, dentistry, veterinary medicine or veterinary science and you can only apply to one course at either the University of Oxford or the University of Cambridge, with a few exceptions. Visit the University of Oxford (www.ox.ac.uk) and University of Cambridge (www.study.cam.ac.uk) websites to find out more.

3 Each UK University will review your individual application based on:

- Your education so far and your predicted grades – provided by your teachers.

- Your employment history – if you've had any paid full-time or part-time jobs you can enter details here.

- Your reference – written on your behalf by a teacher, advisor or professional of your choice.

- Your personal statement – written by yourself and outlining why you should be offered a place on the course in question and mentioning any voluntary or unpaid work you have undertaken. Have a look at the 'How to write your personal statement' section on the website if you don't know where to start.

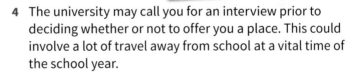

4 The university may call you for an interview prior to deciding whether or not to offer you a place. This could involve a lot of travel away from school at a vital time of the school year.

5 You may receive a conditional offer on one or more of your five choices based on you securing specific grades in named Leaving Certificate subjects.

6 You must then nominate one course, plus a reserved course as a back-up.

7 If you reach the grades required the course is yours. If you don't, depending on the overall acceptance rate from other applicants, you may still get a place on a lower result than the one agreed.

8 Most universities will decide by early May whether or not they're making an offer.

9 Unfilled places still available after the initial round of offers and acceptances go into a 'Clearing' process which is like a market. In August anyone can apply for a place available in this 'Clearing' process.

Your UCAS Action Plan

If you are intending to submit a UCAS application you need to check the website for the exact due date in January and start preparing your application this month. It's important that you take action on the following:

1 Get all of your documents organised.

2 Talk to your teachers about your predicted grades.

3 Ask whichever teacher or advisor you feel knows you best, and who will give you the best possible written reference (not always the same person), to write one for you to be delivered on an agreed date.

4 Practise writing your personal statement, making sure it is within the required number of characters.

5 When you have a draft statement that you are happy with, review it with your guidance counsellor or some other adult whose writing skills and judgment you trust, e.g. your English teacher.

6 Applying early is advisable but students who submit an application by 6 p.m. on the closing date, e.g. 15 January, are guaranteed equal consideration by universities and colleges.

7 Many universities and colleges offer extended deadlines for international applicants – you can check this directly with the institutions.

8 You can apply to many courses at the same time so that your chances of getting a place somewhere are increased. You need to keep in mind that applications are quite competitive, especially for the most popular courses.

If you get ready now you will be able to submit your application when you get back to school in the second week of January. Otherwise you will be in a total panic, asking teachers to provide vital documents for you 'yesterday!' – not a very good idea!

If your school handles a lot of UCAS applications it will have a school code and all applications will be submitted by the school on your behalf. If, as in most schools, only a handful of students ever apply to UCAS you may have to submit an individual application. The fee is Stg£12 for a single course choice or Stg£23 for up to five course choices.

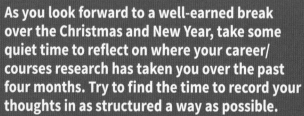

As you look forward to a well-earned break over the Christmas and New Year, take some quiet time to reflect on where your career/ courses research has taken you over the past four months. Try to find the time to record your thoughts in as structured a way as possible.

Application deadlines in Ireland, the UK, Europe, and further afield, will begin to pile up early in the New Year. It would be very helpful over the coming months if you use the Christmas break to sketch out an initial career/ courses plan of action for yourself. Do it now before your Mocks, your orals and your aurals begin to dominate your thoughts.

EXTRA! EXTRA!

Moving Abroad

I'd love to say that my move to den Haag (The Hague, Netherlands), was planned well in advance. That I had everything sorted months before I was due to leave and was fully equipped to take on the challenge of moving country. This was not the case.

It's probably best that I say a bit about the mindset I was in before I moved, and why it was the best decision I have ever made.

I completed my Leaving Cert in 2012, and let's just say my results meant I was not going to be doing Medicine in Trinity. I got offered my tenth choice and embarked on my third level education in September 2012. At the beginning I enjoyed it, but after three months it was clear to my parents and to myself that I was unhappy.

I dropped out in December and began working full-time for a company at the beginning of 2013. I loved my time there and learnt a huge amount, but I was always going to go back to college. After re-sitting maths and re-applying to the CAO, I was devastated that yet again, I was offered my tenth choice.

At this stage I felt lost. I was not too optimistic about my future and felt concerned that I would not be getting the full 'college experience' by sticking around in Dublin, going to the same clubs and cafés every day and night. This mindset changed quite rapidly when my mom came home and told me about a website she had heard about on the radio. It was called EUNiCAS, and it's a bridging point for Irish and British students who wish to study in mainland Europe (or even Scandinavia).

I immediately clicked on and had a browse. Even though it was August, there were still courses available in places like the Netherlands, France, Sweden, Spain, Italy and Norway. The fees were surprisingly low, with the average costing about €1,800 (€700 less than Irish fees, which are currently on the rise).

I noticed one particular course, European Studies,

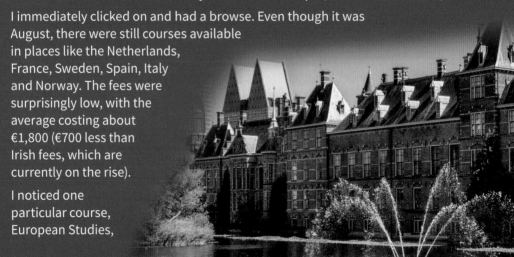

which was offered in The Hague University of Applied Sciences. It was a mix of politics and business, which was right up my alley. I was very excited. Not only was the course something that I would be interested in, but it was in another country. Also, the entry requirements for getting into a Dutch university are not that high, a few C grades and a B and you're in.

I weighed up the pros and cons. On the one hand, I could stay in Dublin, and live the same life I had been living for years. Or, I could take the plunge and move to The Hague, with no friends or knowledge of the city. I also looked at it from a CV point of view, and how impressive a degree from another country would be. There were just far too many pros, and I felt that if I turned down this opportunity, I would regret it forever.

Three weeks after my mom came home and mentioned the possibility of studying abroad, I was on a flight to the Netherlands. I had two massive suitcases full of clothes and a folder containing all my documents. I was scared, nervous, excited, and a bit baffled that within three weeks I had decided to leave Ireland. I love Ireland, but it's a small place. After a while everything is the same, and you begin to feel trapped. Ironically the Netherlands is smaller than Ireland, but I was going there with a clean slate. I was attempting something new and different, forcing myself to live in a country that I knew very little about.

I must have looked quite strange to the Dutch when I first arrived, looking around in wonderment with two suitcases and several sheets of paper in my hands. But to me, it was a sense of adventure, something few of my friends were doing (some moved to the UK, but none to a non-English speaking country, though the Dutch speak amazing English).

The first few weeks were a mixed bag. Because I arrived in September, I had missed the introduction weeks and felt very lost. Luckily I got some wonderful help and managed to find out my timetable, and what books I needed. My accommodation was arranged just before I left Ireland. I moved to a big student building which had a shopping centre in front of it and my college two minutes away. I had to adjust to being back in college, attending 9 a.m. lectures and doing homework. I had to register with the city council, get health insurance and generally just do a lot of things. It was a challenging time. I missed home, as anyone would. I missed not having to cook for myself and not having to do the food shopping.

But my first few months in The Hague taught me so much. I became more independent, more certain of my decisions, and it made me more of an adult. I explored the city and read up on its history. What was most surprising was how laid back the Dutch are. I walked through the Dutch parliament several times before I realised. The pace is slower than Dublin, but not so slow that shops are closed early or there isn't any nightlife.

I began making friends and getting out more. The Hague is a classic 'European' city – squares with people enjoying a coffee or beer and everyone is well dressed. I cannot compliment the Dutch enough on how good their English is. Not only is my course taught through English, but go to any bar, restaurant or café and the moment they realise you can't speak Dutch, they switch to English without any hesitation. I feel very embarrassed that my ability to pick up languages is poor.

Something that has helped me settle in is the Irish community. Go to any city in the world and you are guaranteed to find an Irish pub with an Irish crowd. Not only have I met fellow Irishmen at the pub, but I've even gotten involved with den Haag GAA football team. We train once a week with tournaments held in Amsterdam, Brussels and Luxembourg. You feel so at home when with other Irish people, even small things like saying 'any craic with ya' makes me feel like I'm in Ireland. You can only really say that to an Irish person, as the Dutch will think you mean something very different!

Another fantastic avenue I have discovered is teaching English. Being a native speaker has put me in huge demand. I teach several times a week, earning a decent amount. Move to any city in mainland Europe and you are bound to find people willing to pay you decent money to teach them English. Regardless of what poet came up in the LC and what grade you got, being a native English speaker makes you a very sought after person.

At this stage I should probably mention some difficulties I encountered. Moving country is not plain sailing. The Dutch have a reputation for being very direct, to the point of being just downright rude. I had several arguments on the phone and in person over various things. I either had to ramp up the Irish charm or just get very angry. One example of this was when, just after my dad had paid the fees, I received an email during class that said if I did not present my high school diploma, the college would block my student account. I marched straight down to the administration office and said very firmly that it would not look good on their part if they were to accept money, no problem, but then took issue with not seeing my Leaving Certificate 'diploma'. Why would we pay money if I didn't have a high

school diploma? They eventually saw that I was right and didn't block my student account. Moving country has certainly made me more confident with dealings of an administration matter.

So, to summarise. Moving to The Hague was by far and away the best decision I have ever made. Although the decision was spontaneous, and little research had been made, I realised whilst sipping a coffee overlooking one of the countless Dutch canals, that I had made the right choice.

I love the Netherlands. I love the fact that I'm studying abroad; I love doing something that is different and not 'the norm'. The experiences I have had in my first year have opened my eyes to different cultures, different people, different views and opinions. I feel better equipped to take on future life challenges.

Would I recommend studying in the Netherlands, or another country in Europe? Absolutely yes. Ireland is fantastic and it will always be home, but studying a few years in a different country, with a different way of life and culture, will improve you, not only educationally, but as a human being as well.

The Dutch proverb *Afwisseling verheugt* means 'change enhances' or 'variety pleases'. This could not sum up what studying abroad means any better.

Danny Ryan
The Hague,
The Netherlands

5 January

- The closing date for the CAO 'Early Bird' online application is 20 January. The application fee is €25. The fee increases to €40 after that date until the 1 February deadline. The final date for the standard €115 fee for early applications to the HPAT is also in January.
- Check all relevant EU or International application date deadlines on the colleges' individual websites.
- Royal College of Surgeons Dublin host an Open Day this month and registration closes for the HPAT testing throughout Ireland.
- The UCAS application deadline is 15 January – check its website www.ucas.com for details on the application process and the exact date. You need your finalised personal statement and a reference from your teacher/advisor.
- Many of the Further Education colleges host Open Days including Ballsbridge, Ballyfermot, Bray, Crumlin, Dunboyne, Dun Laoghaire, Marino and Whitehall.
- Check the Dublin Business School, NUI Maynooth, University of Limerick and National College of Ireland for dates on Open Days and CAO Information Evening.
- Limerick IT, Galway-Mayo IT and Dundalk IT run more Open Days this month, including a Portfolio Open Day.

Getting Organised

If you used the Christmas and New Year break to organise your thoughts regarding what course or pathway you will end up taking next September you now have three weeks to make those plans real before the Mocks and orals in February/March.

For many students and parents this can feel like a terrifyingly stressful challenge, as if your entire future career journey will be determined by the decisions you are about to make. Nothing could be further from the truth.

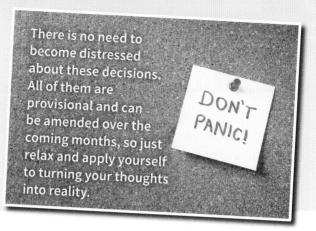

There is no need to become distressed about these decisions. All of them are provisional and can be amended over the coming months, so just relax and apply yourself to turning your thoughts into reality.

DON'T PANIC!

Meet Your Guidance Counsellor

If you can have a one-to-one meeting with a qualified guidance counsellor in school during January take up that opportunity. Make sure to have done all the ground work before the meeting.

If you are a registered 'Reach' user on the Careers Portal website, complete the various exercises on the programme and your guidance counsellor can then explore them with you.

You should also bring all other relevant data to the meeting such as:

- ✓ Examination results, including the ones you may just have received from your teachers.

- ✓ Course and college research you have conducted online.

- ✓ Reflections on work experience or work shadowing you undertook as part of a career exploration.

- ✓ Notes on Open Days you attended in particular colleges or departments.

If you do this work in advance, your guidance counsellor meeting will be very effective.

SPOTLIGHT ON MEDICINE

If you want to apply for a place in an undergraduate medical degree course you could explore the Royal College of Surgeons at its January Open Day. You should also have already made the following preparations:

✓ You will have applied to the CAO to secure a CAO application number, without which you cannot make a HPAT application.

✓ You will have submitted an application to HPAT–Ireland to sit its test which will take place at the end of February/early March in a number of centres around Ireland.

✓ You will have nominated your preferred examination Test Centre. It is important that you take the time to do this as you don't want to end up travelling to the other side of the country because the Centre of your choice is full.

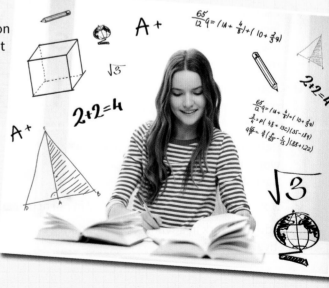

✓ You will have received a number of sample workbooks from HPAT–Ireland and you will have practised each test under examination conditions.

The Health Professions Admission Test (HPAT) Exam

The HPAT exam was introduced to Ireland in 2009, with the declared intention to broaden student access to medical schools. It is an aptitude test designed to assess a candidate's skills in the areas of reasoning, understanding and working with people. These skills have been identified as important attributes for someone who wants to become a competent doctor. The HPAT does not examine academic knowledge but looks at how a person might react in certain situations or how someone might feel. For more information see www.hpat-ireland.acer.edu.au

Many 6th Year students feel that it is essential to take additional grinds in HPAT at a cost of several hundred Euro. ACER, the Australian Council for Educational Research, and publishers of HPAT exams, claim that there is no benefit to be gained by attending such courses. But in a sense they have to say this, as to suggest that the score a student gets in the test could be improved by grinds undermines their claim that the test is a predictor of what makes a good doctor.

Research undertaken by the five Irish Medical schools showed that in the first three years of the HPAT test the numbers securing places as a result of repeating the test was 40 per cent of all successful applicants. Their research also found that Section 3 of the test, Non-Verbal Reasoning, was the one area that showed the greatest level of improved performance, following a repeat year. If you cannot afford expensive revision courses, you need to continuously practise the sample questions provided by HPAT–Ireland, and to seek particular help with the non-verbal reasoning questions.

One positive result of the research finding was that the marking structure of the HPAT test was changed. Sections 1 and 2, Logical Reasoning and Problem Solving and Interpersonal Understanding, are now worth 40 per cent of the overall marks each, with Non-Verbal Reasoning reduced to 20 per cent. This change was introduced in 2014 and the HPAT scores dropped across the board, leading to a one-off reduction of 14–18 points in the requirements for the five medical undergraduate degrees.

Interpreting your HPAT Results

You will not receive the results of your HPAT test until the Monday after you have finished your written Leaving Certificate papers. However, it will still be in plenty of time for you to amend your final list of CAO choices on 1 July.

If you score 180–220 in your HPAT test and believe that you will get a minimum of 550 CAO points in your Leaving Certificate have a very good chance of securing an undergraduate medical place. If your HPAT score falls well short of 180 you should ensure that you have alternative CAO courses listed on your application before the 1July change of mind deadline.

When you receive your Leaving Certificate results in Mid-August you must have a CAO score of over 480 points and meet all of the Medicine matriculation requirements to be eligible for a place in medicine.

If you meet those criteria your CAO score up to 550 points will be added to your HPAT score. The maximum score from HPAT is 300 so that would be a potential 850 points. One extra point can then be added for every five additional CAO points you secure over 550. This is up to the maximum CAO score of 625 which includes the Honours Maths bonus points.

Top Tip!

The results you get in your HPAT can only be used in the current year.

A perfect Medical points score would therefore be **865**:

CAO score: 550 points+

HPAT score: 300 points

Extra CAO points (625 – 550 = 75/5): 15 points

Total points: 865 points

What is EUNiCAS?

EUNiCAS, the European University Central Application Support Service, was set up to assist the ever-increasing numbers of Irish and UK students who cannot access their preferred university course at home. It also helps students whose primary objective is to study abroad.

The EUNiCAS website, www.eunicas.ie, features detailed information on over 240 universities across Continental Europe, listing all the courses they offer that are taught through the English language.

Cambridge Occupational Analysts (COA), the UK's leading careers profiling service, provides an Interest Inventory called Centigrade. It is linked to all CAO, UCAS and EUNiCAS courses, COA has recently added Canadian, Australian & New Zealand degrees to their database.

If you get the opportunity to take the Centigrade test online, your career interests will be identified. You can then select an option to list all relevant courses from any, or all, of the three Irish, UK and EU course databases. In this way you can cut down hugely on the amount of research you need to do.

It is an independent service and does not charge universities for listing their programmes.

You can find details on over 850 courses through EUNiCAS, ranging from a Bachelor in Hospitality Management in Denmark, a Bachelor of Music and Media Management in Finland, to a BA in International Business in Germany and a BA in Archaeology in Poland.

Many of the three and four year courses do not have any tuition fees. Other courses do have fees but they are considerably less than the registration fees charged at many Irish universities, e.g. a Bachelor of Music degree in Belgium with annual tuition fees of €715 or a Doctor of Medicine and Surgery degree in Italy with fees from €650 to €1,730 per year.

Details of all of these courses and the supports needed to secure a place in them are provided on www.eunicas. ie. You can register with the service for €28, giving you access to advice on the best way to apply to up to eight programmes in universities in Continental Europe, within deadline and with all the necessary documents, e.g. personal statement, certificates, letter of recommendations and so on, enclosed.

Points to note

There are many advantages to choosing to study abroad including:

- Availability of places.
- Realistic entry requirements.
- Free or low fees.
- The quality of the education received.

The Head of EUNiCAS, Guy Flouch, is based in Ennis, County Clare, and has twenty years' experience working for third level institutions. He has spent many years advising both students and their parents about career choices and their options for studying abroad. (See pages 154–160 for more information.)

If you are passionate about wanting to become a doctor or a veterinary surgeon but don't think you will score highly enough to secure a place through the CAO or UCAS process, you should consider applying for a place in one of the three Hungarian English language medical schools or one of the other forty-eight programmes on offer elsewhere in Continental Europe. Entry is based on an examination in Chemistry and Biology in Dublin next May, followed by a short interview on the same day.

European Universities: Important Dates

All of the dates below apply to programmes taught through the English language.

Note: *Many of these deadlines are subject to change and there are always exceptions to the rule. Contact www.eunicas.ie for up-to-date information.*

Top Tip!

For Hungarian universities, fees of approximately €10,000 annually apply. You will find more details about these courses on www.studyhungary.ie . Dr Tim O'Leary, a veterinary surgeon in Schull, West Cork, co-ordinates these programmes, alongside entry to veterinary medicine and dentistry in Budapest.

October	Most Dutch programmes open for applications
1 February	Danish applications open
1 February	Application deadline for some but not all Dutch Liberal Arts and Sciences programmes
Mid-February	Application deadline for Finland
February/ March	Applications for most Dutch Physiotherapy programmes close
15 March	Danish applications close for most programmes
15 March	Swedish applications open for international students
Early April	Deadline to apply to Italian Medicine programmes (provisional)
15 April	Swedish applications close
End April	Application deadline for Veterinary Science programmes in Warsaw, Poland & Budapest, Hungary
1 May	Application deadline for many but not all Dutch programmes with a selection procedure
15 July	Application deadline for many programmes in Germany
30 August	Application deadline for most Dutch Universities of Applied Sciences

Your Initial List of CAO Course Choices

You have until 20 January to submit an application to the CAO on www.cao.ie, at the €25 fee. After 20 January the fee increases to €40 until 1 February at 5.15 p.m.

As stated previously, restricted courses should ideally be listed on your Course Choice List by the 31 January deadline, but they can be added in February for a late fee of €10. Your other choices are very much initial ones.

You can totally change these choices over the coming months, so do not get stressed about making them now. In fact, you are entitled to leave your course choices until May/June if you want to do so, a decision taken by several thousand students each year.

My advice would be for you to make an initial attempt at putting your courses in your preferred order. This will help to clarify your thinking before you put the process aside for three months and it may help to motivate you to study.

Choosing a Course

In making your initial choices you should consider the following:

- Only apply for courses for which you know you currently meet the minimum entry requirements. After your Mocks this may change if you drop down a level from Higher to Ordinary, but you can amend your list in May to accommodate this.

- List the courses in the order you actually want them. The biggest mistake students make is to leave out their favourite course because they can't imagine themselves securing the required entry points. Many tears are shed every August over this issue!

- Never list a course for which you have not read the entire course content on www.qualifax.ie. Make sure you read the career progression opportunities so that you know where the course may lead and the potential postgraduate opportunities open to you.

- Follow your own wishes, not those of your parents, grandparents, aunts or uncles. You have to live with the consequences of the choices you make for another sixty-plus years.

- Don't worry about what your friends are doing; it will lead to total disaster if you base your decision on their choices. You will make new friends within weeks of arriving in college, so choose your course according to your own interests.

- Be realistic about costs. If your parents cannot afford to fund you living away from home factor that into your initial choices. But don't just give up on your dream course. You may be one of the 47 per cent of students who will qualify for a grant, or your performance in the Leaving Certificate may secure you one of a number of scholarships on offer from colleges or from the Department of Education and Skills (DES) third level bursary  scheme. This is targeted at DEIS schools and worth €2,000 per year. Read more about these scholarships on pages 184–185.

- Always explore the Level 7/6 course options as they may enable you to progress directly back to the Level 8 higher degree course you actually want, but may not secure the points for next June. (Whatever you do, don't ignore these course options out of fear of what your friends or your Auntie Mary may think!)

- Cover all possible results in your Leaving Certificate – the good, the bad and the indifferent. That's why you are given ten choices on your Level 8 Honours Degrees list and ten further choices on your Level 7/6 list of courses. Every year over 1,000 students who have over 500 points get no offers because they only listed courses with very high points. So be strategic – list your dream course choices on top, your realistic ones in the middle and your rainy day ones as nine and ten. You need a Plan B just in case the exams don't work out as planned. That way you will still have choices to make in August.

Top Tip!

Irish businessman J. P. McManus sponsors a scholarship programme worth over €6,750 per year. It is administered by the DES. See page 185 for more details.

- Try not to list courses in colleges you have not visited. There is more involved in spending three or four years taking a degree programme, than the lecture content. You have to feel right both on the campus and in the surrounding environment.

- Always try and sit down with your guidance counsellor to tease out your choices. The very process of having to explain your particular choices will help clarify why you are picking them. If you can't explain why you are listing a course, this may be a sign that it is not a well thought-out choice.

- Always take your extra-curricular interests into consideration in making your course choices. Look at college clubs, societies, sports teams and so on.

Top Tip!

If you are a high performer in a particular sport or the Arts you may be offered a scholarship which brings financial benefits or in some cases for highly skilled performers in your discipline a reduced points' requirement. See pages 174–177.

- If you are considering a degree programme that involves a year on work placement or a year studying abroad, consider all the implications of such a choice, financial and otherwise, before putting it on your final list of course choices in June.

EXTRA! EXTRA!

CAO TIPS FOR PARENTS/GUARDIANS

Researching Courses

Help your child to research their courses:

1 In the CAO handbook or on the CAO website – watch out for minimum entry requirements.

2 Note any restricted courses, e.g. programmes with early application dates or if an interview is part of the application process.

3 Request a prospectus from the college your son/daughter is most interested in attending or visit its website.

4 Be sure to consider the financial costs involved in the course your son/daughter decides to apply for, such as accommodation, food and travel expenses for the year.

Apply Early

Encourage your son/daughter to apply early using an online application form.

An online application demo is available via **www.cao.ie** from early November. Applying this way has a number of benefits:

1 Candidates can avoid some of the common pitfalls involved, e.g. entering an invalid course code as that would be detected immediately by the CAO system.

2 Applicants receive an acknowledgement email containing details of their registration including course choices and their CAO application number.

3 If your son/daughter sends an application by post they will not receive a Statement of Course Choices – containing their CAO application number, personal information and their course choices – until mid-February.

4 If they have received their application number and want to check if the information they input was recorded correctly, they can login to their account at any time.

Order of Preference

Ensure your son/daughter lists courses in their genuine order of preference.

Your child should not apply based on predictions about how well they expect to do in the Leaving Certificate or on the likely points for the courses they've chosen.

It is important that students realise that they will be offered the single highest preference course on each list for which they are deemed eligible and have the required points.

Points-to-note

Changes to some personal information cannot be carried out online and your child will have to post the amendment with their CAO application number to CAO, Tower House, Eglinton Street, Galway. Keep proof of postage.

Important Deadlines

Watch out for important application deadlines throughout the year. They will be similar to the sample dates below. (Check www.cao.ie for current dates.)

CAO Date	Deadline
5 November 12.00 noon	Online application facility opens
20 January 5.15 p.m.	Discounted online application fee deadline – €25
31 January 5.15 p.m.	Change of Course Choices closes
1 February 5.15 p.m.	Normal closing date for online and paper applications
5 February 12.00 noon	Online facility to amend course choices opens
15 February	Statement of Course Choices sent to paper applicants only
1 March 5.15 p.m.	Closing date for amending course choices
1 April 5.15 p.m.	Latest date for HEAR/DARE documentation to be received by CAO
1 May 5.15 p.m.	Closing date for late applications
5 May 12.00 noon	Online Change of Mind facility becomes available
15 May	Late paper applicants sent a Statement of Course Choices
End of May	Statement of Application Record sent to all applicants
1 July 5.15 p.m.	Change of Mind closes
22 July 5.15 p.m.	Exceptional closing date

CAO Correspondence

Remind your child to review all CAO correspondence very carefully.

- The CAO communicates with applicants via e-mail, text and post at different stages throughout the year. All correspondence from the CAO should be treated as extremely important and checked carefully to make sure that the information held on file is correct.

- Before the end of May all applicants (online and paper) will receive a Statement of Application Record and a Change of Mind Form in the post.

- The Change of Mind (restrictions apply) facility is available online and most students will make their changes there. Consult the CAO website for amendment deadlines and for restrictions on introducing courses.

- The best method for getting in touch with the CAO is via its website. Use the online system, quoting your child's application number – you must have this number – and the CAO will review your son/daughter's file and revert with an answer to the query in writing within one working day. You can also call the CAO on 091 509800, but the phone lines are extremely busy.

Accepting an Offer

Make sure your son/daughter returns offer acceptance notices on time. There are four main rounds of offers:

Round A (early July)

Deferred applicants; mature applicants; mature nursing/midwifery code applicants; and applicants who have completed an Access course.

Round Zero (early August)

Graduate entry medicine applicants; additional mature, deferred and Access applicants; and applicants for entry to courses with a quota for FETAC applicants (now replaced by Quality and Qualifications Ireland).

Round One (mid-August)

All applicants applying on the basis of school leaving examination results, regardless of year completed.

Round Two (late August – mid-October)

After Round One offers have been accepted subsequent offers are issued by the CAO as necessary until October to fill any vacancies that may arise.

If your child is entitled to an offer they will receive an Offer Notice by post and offers will also be available online. Check that all the details are correct.

- If your child receives and decides to accept an offer, they can do so online. They can only accept one offer from either their Level 8 or their Level 7/6 list. Your son/daughter will receive an acknowledgment e-mail and they can also check that their acceptance has been recorded. They will also receive formal notification by post within three working days after the Reply Date. If this does not arrive the CAO should be contacted.

- Accepting an offer in Round One does not mean that your child may not receive an offer of a place on a higher preference course in subsequent offer rounds. If a place becomes available, your son/daughter can choose to accept the new offer, automatically cancelling the previous acceptance.

- If your child decides to defer an offer they must write/e-mail **immediately** to the College Admissions Office, marking Deferred Entry on the envelope/subject line. Students must give their name, CAO application number, the course code and set out their reason(s) for deferral. The letter/e-mail must arrive at least two days before the 'Reply Date' shown on the Offer Notice. The college will communicate their decision to your child. If the deferral is not granted, your child may then accept the offer for the current year, providing they return their acceptance notice within the agreed deadline.

6 February

- 1 February is the closing date for CAO applications of initial course choices to include ALL possible restricted application course choices. The application fee from 20 January to 1 February initial closing date is €40. If you decide during February that you want to add a restricted application course to your existing list of course choices, you may do so by paying an additional €10 after 5 February. This facility closes on 1 March.

- HEAR/DARE applicants need to indicate by 1 March, that they wish to be considered for either or both schemes on their CAO application record. They have to complete all elements of the online application form by that date. Applicants then have a further month to source all necessary paperwork, including medical consultants' reports and evidence of family income, and submit to the CAO offices by the 1 April deadline.

- HPAT applicants need to finalise all practice tests. Registrations for HPAT close at 5.15 p.m. on 1 February, with payment of an additional late fee of €70 due for those paying after 20 January, on top of the registration fee of €115. An exceptional late registration is usually available over the following few days, on payment of the exceptional late fee of €105, plus the €115 registration fee. Check www.cao.ie for more information.

- If you submit a paper application form, you should have received a Statement of Course Choices from the CAO by 15 February. This document provides you with your CAO application number and sets out the courses that you have listed in your initial application.

- Portfolios need to be ready for presentation in relevant subject areas: art, music, architecture, drama, photography and so on. For example, the National College of Art and Design portfolio submission deadline is early February.

- This is the month when the Post Leaving Cert (PLC) colleges come into their own. Open Days and interviews with Killester/Ormonde/Dunboyne Colleges of Further Education (CFE) take place this month.

- In February each year the ESB normally advertises for apprentice electricians. As you would expect, competition for these places is intense. You will be notified of this and any other relevant apprentice/career opportunities on the www. careersnews.ie website.

- Use your Mid-Term Break to review your progress and make sure that you are on target to meet all application deadlines in your career planning process. Don't allow yourself to drift towards applying just before the closing dates with the expectation that somebody else will sort it out for you at the last minute.

As the month of February progresses the feeling that you are in the departure lounge of second level education intensifies. You are most likely sitting your Leaving Certificate Mocks this month, which brings this reality even more firmly home to you. You may also be working hard to submit project work which is an assessable component of some of your Leaving Certificate subjects, and your orals in Irish and the other continental languages you are studying are only weeks away.

You may be completely content with your career progression plans at this stage of the year, having already applied for courses through the CAO, UCAS or EUNiCAS. You could, however, be considering other options.

Career Journey Options Outside Third Level

Every year over 12,000 current Leaving Certificate students do not apply to the CAO seeking a college place. If you are one of these students you probably do not see your career prospects being initially advanced through third level education. There are a number of possible reasons for this:

- You would prefer to move directly into the labour market and are starting to work on your Curriculum Vitae (CV) and introductory letter. (See pages 144–151 for more information.)
- You want to take a one-year Post Leaving Certificate course that will give you the basic skills necessary to secure an entry level position with an employer.

- You want to secure an apprenticeship within a trade or craft and have no interest in further academic studies. Many thousands of 6th Year students pursue this route and do not continue academic studies unless they are an essential aspect of securing their trade or craft qualification.

- You feel that you are not ready to commit to a CAO course in the current year or you do not expect to secure enough points through the Leaving Certificate. If you are in this situation you can explore various PLC course options on www.careersportal.ie. Attending appropriate PLC Open Days will also help you to make a decision. (See pages 141–143 for more information.)

Top Tip!

If you can identify with any of these scenarios, now is the time to begin to put in place a plan to realise your goals.

Points to note

Now that the construction industry has begun to recover throughout the country, new opportunities may arise for school leavers to secure apprenticeships. Traditional apprenticeships are still available, if you can secure the endorsement of a registered tradesperson in the electrical, motor, engineering and printing trades. As new building projects start to get off the ground in February this is the right time of year to locate a qualified tradesperson in your area to see if they are prepared to offer you a standards based apprenticeship. (See pages 152–156 to learn more about Apprenticeships.)

Top Tip!

What is SUSI? SUSI, www.susi.ie, is the national awarding authority responsible for working out if you are eligible for a Student Grant and what assistance you might be entitled to. This could be useful information as you make your CAO course choices. (See pages 119–122 for more information.)

How Are the CAO Points Determined?

1 The final list of applicants for each course offered through the CAO application process is finalised at 5.15 p.m. on 1 July next. A full list of applicants is drawn-up for each course. This list may be added to by the addition of current undergraduate students who drop out of their existing course and apply for a new one, up to mid-July.

2 When the Leaving Certificate results are released in mid-August the grades for each student who has applied for a college place are entered into his/her CAO record.

3 Each list of course applicants is then re-ordered with the student who has 625 points at the top of the list.

4 Within a day or so the admissions officers from all the colleges meet with the CAO and inform them of the exact number of places to offer on each course. This can range from 1,200 places for an Arts degree in UCD to less than 10 places in many highly specialised course codes. Students with high points who are offered these courses will probably find themselves in lecture theatres with approx. 300–400 other students, many of whom secured places on more general courses, requiring much lower points.

College representatives may also instruct the CAO to add points to scores by specific applicants to some courses, as a consequence of a successful HEAR/DARE application, or their equivalent in colleges outside these schemes.

Additional points may also be added to CAO scores by applicants whom the colleges deem elite sportspersons, musicians and performers and who qualify for a scholarship on that basis. (See pages 174–177 for more information.)

Top Tip!
All CAO applicants will be offered a course choice higher up their list of choices if it becomes available following the non-acceptance of offers by other candidates. This will happen even if you have already accepted another lower choice offer.

5 Once all the adjustments have been made to the application list for each course, based on each applicant's results and on the confirmed places on offer, the CAO computer then allocates places.

6 All applicants who have applied for courses are offered the highest choice to which their points entitle them, on both their Level 8 Higher Degree and Level 6/7 Higher Certificate/Ordinary degree list.

7   If you restrict your CAO application to a small number of high points courses and you are under the cut-off point for all of them, you will not receive a course offer at this stage.

It is imperative that you list all your course choices in the order that you actually desire them, from 1 to 10. Option 1 must be the course you want the most and option 10 should be the course you desire least.

What Determines the Points for Courses Each Year?

Will the points' requirement for most course increase this year?

Nobody knows what the points requirement for any particular course will be this year or any year for that matter. This is for the following reasons:

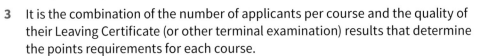

1   Up until the 1 July close of applications, the number of candidates who apply for each course is unknown.

2   Until the Leaving Certificate results are released in mid-August, the quality of the results and consequentially the CAO points score are also unknown.

3   It is the combination of the number of applicants per course and the quality of their Leaving Certificate (or other terminal examination) results that determine the points requirements for each course.

4   Colleges have no role whatsoever in setting points for courses, other than in determining the number of places they offer on each programme. A course with 1,000 places, such as an Arts degree, will have lower points than a small programme, offering five places.

CAO – Applying by Snail Mail

If you are one of a tiny minority of applicants who intend to return a paper application to the CAO by post it must be in its Galway offices by 5.15 p.m. on 1 February. You will then receive a Statement of Course Choices in mid-February next, which will show your allocated CAO application number, as well as the course choices that the CAO has entered onto your file. This statement should arrive by post. If it does not, you must contact the CAO immediately. If you don't you could be excluded from some course choices.

It is very important that you check the course choices listed in your Statement of Course Choices immediately to ensure that they are correct.

Points to note

Applicants wishing to apply for undergraduate medical degrees cannot use the paper application system. You will need a CAO application number to apply for HPAT by the initial 20 January deadline. As a paper applicant you won't get this number from the CAO until 1 February, by which time it is of no use to you.

Students who apply online will not be sent a Statement of Course Choices, as the purpose of this document is to inform applicants of their application number, and to allow them to make course changes after applying.

February Focus: CAO – Change of Mind

You have the month of February to change your initial choices, if you wish.

Between 5 February next and 1 March, any applicant may make a course choice change by paying the additional processing fee of €10 to the CAO at www.cao.ie.

This applies to categories including if you:

- Are a mature student.
- Wish to apply for an additional restricted application course(s).
- Want to correct or amend your application record.

If you are not in the categories mentioned above, <u>you do not need to correct any course errors at this stage</u>. Instead you can wait until 1 May and make any course changes for free. You may use this Change of Mind facility between 1 May and 1 July.

CAO – Key Mistakes

What are the key mistakes applicants make each year?

✓ **Failure to fully read the CAO handbook,** particularly the detailed rules and regulations of the process.

✓ **Leaving your application to the last minute:** One applicant did this in 2013, starting an online application at 5.14 p.m. on the closing date. How daft is that?

✓ **Not fully researching your course choices:** You need to know the content and entry requirement of the courses you list.

✓ **Failure to allow for a lower points score in your Leaving Certificate results:** Over 1,000 students who score over 500 points each year receive no offers.

✓ **Forgetting to read and respond to correspondence from the CAO:** A typical excuse, 'I had too much going on in my life to bother opening the envelope.'

✓ **Deciding not to apply for the course you actually want. Many students don't list their top course** because they underestimate how well they may do in their Leaving Certificate.

- ✓ **DARE applicants forgetting to return ALL of the required documentation:** You must have letters from appropriate medical consultants ready to send to the CAO in time for the 1 April due date.

- ✓ **HEAR applicants failing to return support documentation:** If you are applying for HEAR you need to supply evidence of family income by the 1 April due date.

- ✓ **Early round applicants not responding to offers in the first week of July and early August** because of unattended post during the peak holiday season. The excuse given is often that there is no media coverage of these rounds of CAO offers. If you are on holidays the offers can be responded to online.

This situation will apply to you if you secure a college place this year and secure a 'Deferral'. You must then re-apply to the CAO next year, listing only your deferred course, and you will receive your offer both online and by post in the first week of July.

It will also apply to you if you do a PLC course next year and apply to the CAO seeking a place based on your PLC results. You will probably receive your offer on 1/2 August.

- ✓ **Failure to use the full capacity of the twenty choices on offer:** If you make no course choices from the Level 6/7 options, even though many of these courses have progression routes into the Level 8 courses, you have no Plan B if you do not get enough points in your Leaving Certificate grades for a Level 8 offer.

- ✓ **Applying to a college or course because it is where your friends are going.** Instead you need to focus on selecting the right course for you and you will make new friends quickly.

Top Tip!

The biggest mistake you can make is to believe that going to college in the year following your Leaving Certificate is a given. Sometimes a year out to reflect on what you want to do or taking a one year Post Leaving Certificate course might be a far more appropriate choice.

EXTRA! EXTRA!

Name: Cathal

Programme: Level 7 Business Management

CAO Application: When I was doing my Leaving Cert I went through a very tough time personally and my academic performance suffered massively. I feel that if I had been made aware of all of the options open to me, not just the university Level 8 route, I may have been able to refocus myself and pursue a PLC course or Level 6/7 option rather than thinking I had no options.

Points: I sat a very bad Leaving Certificate and thought that most of my options for college were gone. I had always wanted to be a teacher and in the absence of any other options, I chose to do hairdressing which I excelled at and eventually became a teacher in a prestigious hair dressing school.

Plan B: With the downturn in the economy I was made redundant. It was then that I decided to pursue my original dream of becoming a teacher. Unlike when I was in my Leaving Certificate year, I did some in-depth research into the various options available.

Course: Having come from quite a middle-class school environment we were encouraged to move onto the university path, whether or not it was what suited our individual needs. I was not made aware of the PLC courses available or of the benefits associated with the ladder progression entry system (Level 6, 7 and 8) offered by ITs. Not that I regret going down the route of hairdressing. It was something I was very good at and that gave me a substantial confidence boost.

I went back to do a PLC course to reacquaint myself with the experience and practice of learning, preparing essays and so on. I then got accepted on to the Level 6 Business Management course in IT Tallaght. I completed Level 6 and then moved on to Level 7 and have just finished my exams.

Result: I love my course and really enjoy the learning environment in IT Tallaght. I have friends who are studying in universities and they are doing very well but they have classes with 400 people in them and some of their lecturers don't know who they are. The IT system works for me, as I have more access to my lecturers, if and when I need help, and I like the friendly atmosphere. My intention is to progress on to the Level 8 and then move on to do an H. Dip in Teaching, so that I can fulfil my dream of becoming a second level teacher.

Top Tip: I suppose if I had to give a current 6th Year some advice I would say to explore all of your options. Doing a PLC course or entering at a Level 6 won't suit everyone, but it is a good solution for some who maybe aren't certain what they want to do and don't want to commit to a Level 8 course. If you do want to do a Level 8 but there is also a Level 6/7 option, make sure you put it down on your CAO. You never know what could happen during your exams and by listing Level 6 and 7 courses you are just giving yourself more options.

Name: Sinead

Degree: Level 8 Business Enterprise at Institute of Art, Design & Technology (IADT), Dun Laoghaire, Dublin

Plan B: I would recommend the PLC route to any Leaving Certificate student who is seeking an affordable and mainly assignment-based, assessment format that is taught by friendly approachable lecturers.

Course: Two year, full-time Higher National Diploma in Business Studies at Blackrock Further Education Institute (previously Senior College Dun Laoghaire). The HND Business Studies course provided me with a broad spectrum of business knowledge, making me workplace ready for a career in the world of business.

CAO Application: Like many other PLC courses nationwide, on completion of my course I had the opportunity to progress onwards to one of a number of degree options within the higher education system. I did not have to apply through the CAO because *graduates from the HND in Business can complete an internal application form for advanced entry.* In my case, I had the opportunity to achieve an Honours Degree in Business by transferring directly to a number of colleges such as Dublin Business School, IADT and the National College of Ireland.

Result: My experiences on my PLC course over the past two years have been incredibly positive. I have now got the knowledge I need, and also the confidence, to progress my education within the CAO system. I thought about what to do next for a good few weeks and got great help and support from my college's guidance counsellor. In the end I decided to link into the third year of a four-year Honours Degree, Level 8 programme in Business Enterprise at the Institute of Art, Design & Technology (IADT) in Dun Laoghaire, Dublin.

Top Tip: I would highly recommend anyone that is interested in pursuing their studies beyond the Leaving Certificate but may not feel ready to proceed directly onto a CAO course, or is not in a position to do so, to check out the range of courses available at your local PLC College. I also found the full list of all colleges on Qualifax.ie very helpful.

7 March

MARCH FOCUS

PLAN AHEAD

- CAO – 1 March at 5.15 p.m. is the closing date for indicating on your CAO online application that you wish to apply for either HEAR or DARE and to fully and correctly complete all elements of either application forms in your application record.
- Check out the Colleges of Further Education for Enrolment Days and Open Days this month, including Ballsbridge CFE, Westport CFE, Ormonde CFE, Templemore CFE and Killester CFE.
- Agricultural Colleges at Ballyhaise, Clonakilty, Gurteen, Kildalton, Mountbellew and Pallaskenry have Open Days this month.
- CAO – 1 March is the closing date for applicants wishing to amend their course choices to add a restricted application course(s). An additional payment of €10 is levied.
- The College of Amenity Horticulture – Botanic Gardens have an Open Day this month.
- Open Days are held at various Institutes of Technologies and Further Education this month including Athlone, Bray, Carlow and Cork.
- The usual application deadline for UCAS applications is 15 January. But application deadlines for some art and design courses fall towards the end of March. As with the January deadline, your reference must be completed before you can submit your application.

Your Mocks

The most valuable aspect of sitting your Mocks is the actual physical and emotional experience of having to take the full range of your Leaving Certificate papers over a two-week period. This endurance test is a vitally important preparation for the 2–3 weeks of exams you will have to undertake in June – while performing at your best throughout.

Your Results

You may have received your Mock results this month. The results are very important for a number of reasons:

1. They are the first overall indication of your likely performance in your Leaving Certificate, across all of your subjects. However your teachers' interpretation of the results needs to be factored into any conclusions you reach. For example, if the entire class receive grade C/D results the teacher may well say the marking has been too strict, or if everybody receives A/B grades that could also be an issue.

2. They have clarified what you do not know. You have plenty of time over the next three months to focus on specific subject areas to rectify this situation before you have to sit your written papers in June.

3. They give you an insight into how the marking schemes which will be applied to your real Leaving Certificate papers will operate. The marking of your mock exam papers cannot be up to the standards set by the State Examination Commission, so don't waste your energy complaining about the quality of marking. Read through each marked script and take on board any comments written by the external examiner who corrected your script or by your own subject teachers. Remember they go through the process of interpreting mock papers every year.

4. The results may not be as good as you expected. If they are much lower than you thought they would be in some subjects, you should talk to your teachers and take their advice about the appropriate level of paper that you should sit in June.

You may feel frustrated with some of your results but remember that no one will ever ask or remember how you did in the Mocks. They are only a practice run that will ultimately be of huge benefit to you if you take on board the lessons to be learnt from the entire process.

Your Career Plan and the Mocks

What are the implications of your Mock Results for your career planning process?

After you have analysed the results from your Mocks and realistically assessed the level of improvement you can achieve between now and June, calculate your optimum as well as your realistic points' target. With these points in mind review your career/course plans to date.

- Are your Level 8 or Level 6/7 course choices still realistic? Do you need to change them?

- Have you decided to drop from higher to ordinary level in a subject where securing a higher level C or D was a basic entry requirement for a course on your current college application record? If so, you must remove it when you next review your course choices.

- Do you need to review all your options? If you do, make an appointment with your school's guidance counsellor. If you have decided to focus on a new course area before your meeting review ALL courses available on www.qualifax.ie, or if you are now looking beyond Ireland check out www.eunicas.ie. If you do this basic research your guidance counsellor can use every minute of your interview to help direct you concerning any adjustments you should make to your career/course planning process.

> ## Point to note
> If you need to explore some new options you will find that admissions officers in colleges will be only too happy to facilitate your questions as they deal with this scenario in March every year following the Mocks. But whatever you do, do not get distracted away from your studies by this process.

Dealing with Stress

If you are not experiencing some level of stress by now you are in serious trouble. Nobody who is facing the final examination of their school life, after so many years progressing through the system, can avoid being stressed. Stress can in fact be a driver, helping you to find the energy to work effectively and perform to your maximum ability – but only if it is managed through these final twelve weeks.

Positive Management of Stress

The most effective way of managing stress is to devise a study plan covering the run-up to the Leaving Certificate itself. This is not a 100 metre sprint, but a marathon, so every aspect of your life is involved, including diet, sleep, recreation, sport, nutrition, school work, study, rest and relaxation. Sit down and plan out your programme of work over the final weeks before the exams, taking account of all the elements outlined above.

On the State Examinations Commission (SEC) website (www.examinations.ie) you have access to every Past Paper and Answer Scheme for every question you may wish to revise. So use these resources to your full advantage as you prepare for your exams. Make sure that you are absolutely clear about the structure and layout of every paper – the compulsory sections, the weighting of the marks within the sections

of each question, the appropriate amount of time you should allocate to each question and so on.

Once you get your timetable or schedule organised and can clearly see the roadmap you have constructed from now to the date of your final written paper, your perfectly normal levels of stress and tension should begin to subside. If they do not, try some of the following:

- Simple relaxation exercises. Try and do these exercises in the privacy of your own room when you have peace and quiet. If you find this difficult to organise find a quiet spot in a local park or by the sea or river where you can take time apart. Consult your doctor first if you are in any doubt about your fitness levels.

1 Sit comfortably in a straight-backed chair in your room, keeping your back straight, focus on your breathing: breathe in deeply, followed by a slow exhaling of breath to reduce stress.

2 Following the exercise above, scrunch-up every group of muscles in your body in sequence, as you breathe in and hold that tension for a few seconds, before breathing out and relaxing the muscles completely. Do this exercise starting in your left foot and working your way up and down your body into your right foot. You should find this exercise very relaxing.

- A good walk or run can often help to burn-off excess tension.
- If none of these exercises work for you and you find yourself overwhelmed by the stress building up in you to the point where it is interfering with your capacity to study for your examination and with your sleep pattern, make an appointment with your doctor. They may be able to advise you or, in exteme cases, to prescribe some gentle relaxation medication. Never self-administer any medication without seeking your GP's advice beforehand.

March Focus – Review Your Progress

✓ For both DARE and HEAR applications the end of March is the final date for the submission of supportive documentation such as medical consultants' reports and proof of income statements. Applications cannot be considered if any of this documentation is missing or not signed by the appropriate person, holding the specified medical qualification. So be sure to read the literature supplied by www.acesscollege.ie website very carefully.

✓ Students applying to colleges in the UK or Northern Ireland will have attended their various interviews by now and will be considering any offers made to them. If you are in that situation you will have to choose which 'course offer provisional' you wish to accept and which one to nominate as your back-up course.

✓ Students looking to EU university options need to concentrate on the application closing dates as these vary greatly throughout the continent. Again check www.eunicas.ie. Its moderator, Guy Flouch, is an expert in this field and has very good working relationships with all of the Continental Universities, so send him an email if you are unsure of any application closing dates.

✓ The end of March and early April is also a time when many colleges consider and respond to students who have applied for the various scholarship programmes. These scholarships can provide a range of supports including financial supports.

A Little Something For All You Creative Souls Out There

When I was in the same place as you are now, all I wanted to do was to get as far away from school as possible and to start to earn some real money. I did not have a clue what I wanted to do, but given my father's business background I sensed that I would probably start working with him in our family business, which is what I ended up doing initially.

I had a teacher who did not see the best in me and predicted that I would end up digging ditches, to which I replied that whatever I did I would not be coming to work on a bicycle, wearing the same threadbare trousers daily. I predicted to him that one day I would arrive back to visit the school in a Porsche or a Mercedes. This was a huge motivator for me and I relished the day I did drive up to that same school less than ten years later, driving my own brand new Porsche.

How did I get from that dressing down by my teacher to arriving back in some style? My parents were I believe very wise and enlightened in giving me the time and latitude to find my true career path. I started work with my father in the grocery business, and although it did not excite me greatly, he taught me the value of always doing any job properly, no matter how menial. That was a huge learning curve for me. If I was to pass on two key insights that my parents have taught me, it would be to have a singular, healthy positive attitude to any challenge or task you find yourself given, and to give your son/daughter the latitude to find their true calling in life.

One day lounging around at home as all teenagers do my life changed completely and totally by accident, when I picked up a magazine and read an article about this fellow

called Vidal Sassoon. He had been flown over to New York for the sole purpose of cutting Mia Farrow's hair for a movie called 'Rosemary's Baby,' directed by the legendry Roman Polanski. The title of the article was 'The Two Thousand Dollar Haircut'. In the article he was surrounded by beautiful women who were clients of his.

In that moment, at the ripe old age of seventeen, I realised that this was the life for me. I thought to myself that the heaviest thing I was ever going to have to lift was a comb and scissors, and that I was going to live the rest of my life surrounded by beautiful women. Within weeks, through a family friend I found myself in London on a week's holiday. Following my dream I took a chance and cold-called Vidal Sassoon's salon in Bond St from a phone box, looking for an opportunity to start an apprenticeship in hairdressing. As luck work would have it I convinced the girl at the other end of the telephone to give me a chance to begin to fulfil that dream.

When I walked into that salon in 171 New Bond Street and experienced the energy and excitement it was overwhelming. At that precise moment I realised where my future lay. So when the question was put to me ten or fifteen minutes later in a very plush office as to how long I had wanted to do lady's hairdressing, I heard myself saying, 'I have always wanted to be a hairdresser,' and thus my career in hairdressing started.

When I walked out onto the street and met my friend Andy who had brought me there I turned around and looking back at the salon I said to him, 'One day I am going to manage that shop' and thankfully in the fullness of time, at the tender age of twenty-two I did.

But, the pathway to my success stared with probably the most menial job you can imagine – cleaning the toilets in the Salon. My first reaction was to say that I was not raised to clean toilets, but before I did so I remembered the example and training of my parents, and, unpleasant as it may have been, I rolled up my sleeves and did the job like it had never been done before. My diligence was quickly noticed and my career as a hairdresser took off. Within weeks I stood beside my first model with a pair of scissors in my hand and my journey as a hairdresser had really started. Within three months I had won a major competition among all forty apprenticeships in Sassoon's organisation for, ironically, a Mia Farrow lookalike haircut.

Looking back now, following a wonderful career of over forty years in hairdressing I have a simple message for those of you who may aspire to having a successful career in this business. If you feel that you may have a creative talent, have an outgoing personality, have an eye for the Arts, enjoy meeting people rather than sitting in an office, have good hand-eye co-ordination and are prepared to really work hard on honing your skills, the creativity will come.

That creativity along with a pair of scissors in your pocket will take you all around the world, as it did Vidal Sassoon in his day. My former students are working in every corner of the world in well paid jobs. Many of them have moved on as I did to owning their own salons and managing their own business. But for me all of those benefits pale into insignificance compared to the satisfaction that using your skills in cutting and shaping a head of hair can bring.

A great haircut can transform a client and give them a renewed sense of confidence and wellbeing. Your reward is the satisfaction of knowing that the job has been well done, that the client has total confidence in your ability to make them look and feel the very best that they can be and that they leave your store with their head held high for all the world to see.

David

David Marshall manages the David Marshall School of Hairdressing at 27 South Great Georges Street and 12 Fade Street, Dublin 2. See www.davidmarshall.ie and marshalldavid@eircom.net if you are interested in a career in hairdressing and would like more information.

8 April

APRIL FOCUS

- The deadline for all HEAR and DARE documentation to be physically in the CAO offices in Galway is 5.15 p.m. on 1 April.
- Check out dates for Spring Open Days at University College Cork, NUI Galway, NUI Maynooth, Sligo IT and Galway-Mayo IT.
- Interviews and Open Days take place throughout May in Ormonde CFE, Killester CFE, Dun Laoghaire Institute of Art, Design & Technology and the Open Training College.
- Music Entrance tests take place in the Cork Institute of Technology.
- The SciFest exhibition takes place in the Institutes of Technology in Athlone, Cork, Limerick and Waterford.

With just two months to go to the Leaving Certificate your focus this month should rightly be on your revision schedule for the forthcoming examinations. Some of you, however, may be involved in interviews, tests or presentations associated with restricted application courses, scholarship programmes, or the process of securing your place in a UK or other college elsewhere in the world.

Options for Post Leaving Certificate Employment

For many students the world of school and study will end on the day their Leaving Certificate finishes. If that is your goal and you are hoping to find a job after you finish your examinations in June, it is vitally important that you understand the range of

> I want to find a job and start earning a living as quickly as possible after the Leaving Cert!

services and supports that are available to you through the Department of Social Protection (DSP) (**www.welfare.ie**). Each local office now operates under the Intreo brand name.

Points to note

What is Intreo?

Intreo is a one-stop shop for all employment and income supports. You can get job-seeking advice, information on vacancies and help with any questions you may have about your entitlements to jobseeker's payments, back to work and back to education payments or other social welfare payments. For any student in 6th Year considering entering the labour market directly from school the supports available through your local Intreo office will be invaluable.

Intreo personnel offer you expert help and advice on employment, training and personal development opportunities. Their focus will be on you and your needs to help you enter the workforce, and you will also have access to self-service kiosks.

Your Pathway to Work

Services and supports to help you in your job search:

- **Getting a PPSN** – you will need a Personal Public Service Number (PPSN) to register with Intreo/Employment Services. Your PPS number is a unique reference number that helps you access financial supports, public services and information. Only the Department of Social Protection can provide you with a PPS number. To find out more go to **www.welfare.ie** and search for PPSN and how to apply.

- **Employment Services** – you can access details of job vacancies registered with the Department of Social Protection (DSP) at any Intreo Centre and Employment Service Office, locations listed on **www.welfare.ie** and on **www.jobsireland.ie** or on the touch screen kiosks in any local Intreo/Employment Service Office. If you have registered with Intreo/Employment Services, you can also use the freephone service 1800 611 116.

- **A Guidance Interview** – this is an interview with an Employment Officer/Case Officer about employment opportunities, training courses and other services that may help you find work.

- **Local Employment Services (LES)** – these are a full range of services and facilities that are available to help jobseekers. For example, LES staff can support you through guidance interviews, by helping you to develop a career plan and in identifying job opportunities. They can also assist you in identifying training and educational supports.

- **Job Clubs** – provide a drop-in-service, one-to-one meetings and formal workshops to help jobseekers to assess their options, take steps towards reaching their career goals, and explore and follow-up on employment opportunities. For example, staff will help you to prepare your CV, improve your interview skills and identify job opportunities.

The Youth Guarantee

1. If you are not planning to pursue a third level college or PLC course but want to get into the labour market as soon as possible the high levels of youth unemployment in Europe are working to your advantage. In the past year the EU has introduced a Youth Guarantee that applies to all EU citizens who are under twenty-five years of age, whether registered with unemployment services or not.

2. With youth unemployment rates of approximately 26 per cent in 2013, the Irish Government has implemented the youth guarantee scheme. If you have not secured employment, training or an apprenticeship within **four months** of leaving school, the Department of Social Protection (DSP) has committed to providing you with a training or education place. After you have completed your Leaving Certificate in June make sure that you

register with your local DSP office and specify that you are interested in securing a place.

3. This may lead you back to your local Education Training Board and the programmes available to you through their colleges of further education and training. (See pages 141–143 for more information.)

Top Tip!

You can access information on job vacancies through **www.welfare.ie** and **www.jobsireland.ie** which has information about jobs in Ireland and across Europe. Check out public service jobs at **www.publicjobs.ie**.

Jobseeker's Allowance

To get Jobseeker's Allowance you must:

✓ Be fully unemployed or unemployed for at least four days out of seven.

✓ Be over 18 years of age.

✓ Be capable of work.

✓ Be available for and genuinely seeking work.

✓ Satisfy the means test.

✓ Meet the Habitual Residence Condition.

Employment Supports for School Leavers

JobBridge

JobBridge is the National Internship Scheme that provides work experience placements for interns for either six or nine months. The aim of the scheme is to help break the cycle where jobseekers are unable to get a job because they have no experience, either because they are new to the labour market after education or training or they are unemployed workers who want to learn new skills.

To qualify for JobBridge, you must have been claiming one of the following for a total of three months (78 days) or more in the last six months:

- Jobseeker's Allowance
- Jobseeker's Benefit
- One Parent Family Payment
- Disability Allowance

- Signing for credits

The Department of Social Protection will pay you an allowance equivalent to your current social welfare payment plus an additional €50 a week while you are on the scheme. For more information see **www.jobbridge.ie**.

Looking for Jobs through Social Media

Social media sites like Facebook™, LinkedIn™ and Twitter™ can help you find a job and connect with people who can assist you in developing a career. But it's important that the information you post online matches the information on your curriculum vitae (CV). You should also consider who may have access to your online data.

Here are some ways to use your online presence to support your job search.

① Facebook

www.facebook.com

Most people use Facebook to connect with friends or people they know, but you can also use your public Facebook page for networking. Some companies have even created Facebook applications for career searches. The following are examples of useful job seeking Facebook Apps:

1 Jobvite – www.facebook.com/jobvite

This application matches your profile information to jobs in other networks so companies and jobseekers can target each other.

2 BranchOut – www.facebookjob/branchout

This career networking app lets you browse your friends on Facebook to see where they have worked. You can also browse and share jobs that people in your career network have posted and employers can post jobs for free. You can import your LinkedIn profile to BranchOut as well so that you have a professional profile on Facebook.

3 CareerBuilder – www.facebook.com/careerbuilder

With this app information such as your location and career interests are used to send you relevant and up-to-date job and internship postings. You can follow a link directly from the job listing to apply for it. You can also search by keyword, location and category.

4 LinkUp – www.facebook.com/linkup

This app tells you about currently available jobs, searching 40,000+ company websites. Companies can automatically publish jobs from their corporate websites to their Facebook fan pages. Recruitment and advertising agencies are also using this app.

5 BeKnown – www.facebook.com/BeKnownFromMonster

This app is an easy way for you to search for jobs as per normal on Monster.ie without leaving Facebook. So now when you get your job search results you can see who you know at each company. It also lets you keep your personal Facebook information private.

2 LinkedIn

www.linkedin.com

This professional social network has over 300 million members in over 200 countries worldwide and is very useful when you are looking for work. Below are some of the ways you can use it for your job search:

1. **Personal Profile** – with this important feature you can upload your educational background, career details, skills, expertise and interests for employers to review.

2. **Company Search** – you can conduct a search on a company and hopefully find people who are connected to other people you know. You then ask your personal contact to connect you.

3. **Find Jobs** – this feature lets you search for jobs on LinkedIn and also suggests jobs in which you may be interested.

4. **Job Postings** – employers can post jobs on the site at www.linkedin.com/jobs

5. **Email** – you can send an email to everyone in your LinkedIn network.

6. **Blog Link** – you can link your blog post to your LinkedIn profile. Every time you post a new blog, Blog Link updates your profile so people can see what you were writing about. The updated post also goes out in the weekly update emails to your connections.

7. **Endorsements** – friends, colleagues and past colleagues can endorse your work skills and experiences and this will be visible to potential employers.

Useful Apps for Jobseekers to Download

CPL Jobs App for iPhone and Android

EURES Jobs for iPhone

Solas Courses App for iPhone and Android

Glassdoor App for iPhone

Find a Job in Ireland App for iPhone

LinkedIn App for iPhone and Android

Jobseeker App for iPhone and Android

3 Twitter

www.twitter.com

Twitter lets you connect with other users based on your common interests and ideas. Here are some ways to use it for job searches.

Basic Networking – you can link with people who share your interests.

Job Postings – you can follow recruiters and job sites on Twitter to see their job postings (for example @socialmediajob).

Connecting – if you follow someone on Twitter, read their bio thoroughly. If they work somewhere you might be interested in, or if you think they can connect you to others, you can get in touch with them.

Companies – Twitter tools like Twellow can search people's bios and the URLs on their bios. Check out www.twellow.com.

Twitter Job Search – This compiles all jobs on Twitter worldwide. Go to www.twitjobsearch.com and simply type in the job and location you are looking for.

JobAngels – follow this at www.twitter.com/JobAngels for job listings and to help other jobseekers.

JobDeck – download this free app at www.tweetdeck.com/jobdeck to easily search social media for job listings, track the latest job search trends and connect with contacts across Twitter, LinkedIn, Facebook and more.

Tweecal – look this up at www.twitter.com/Tweecal to search for jobs on Twitter by keyword and location.

Twitireland – www.twitireland.com is a directory of Twitter users in Ireland.

Finding a Job in Europe

EURES

The international employment service of the Department of Social Protection is part of the EURES (European Employment Services) Network. EURES was established by the European Commission to assist the free movement of workers between the European Economic Area (EEA) 1 countries.

If you intend to look for a job in Europe when you finish your Leaving Certificate you can use EURES to:

- Access a database of jobs across Europe.
- Access information on living and working conditions in each country.
- Include your CV in a European database which can be viewed by European employers.

This service is free of charge.

EURES has a network of over 800 Advisers across Europe. They provide information, guidance and placement information to both jobseekers and employers interested in the European job market.

> ### Point to note
> ## European Economic Area (EEA) 1 Countries
>
> Austria, Belgium, Bulgaria, Cyprus, Croatia, Czech Republic, Denmark, Estonia, Finland, France, Germany, Greece, Hungary, Iceland, Ireland, Italy, Latvia, Liechtenstein, Lithuania, Luxembourg, Malta, the Netherlands, Norway, Poland, Portugal, Slovak Republic, Romania, Slovenia, Spain, Sweden, Switzerland and the United Kingdom.

The advisers have specialised knowledge in the practical, legal and administrative issues relating to working in another country. They can also access a network of advisers in thirty-two European countries who can respond quickly to specific recruitment enquiries.

If you want more information EURES advisors can be found in Intreo/Employment Services offices throughout Ireland. You can also contact the EURES coordination unit at (01) 673 2702, at eures@welfare.ie or at www.eures.europa.eu.

VOLUNTARY WORK

Voluntary work can be a great way for you to gain valuable work experience when you leave school while also helping a worthwhile cause. Volunteering to work in for example a charity shop, a soup kitchen or a local animal rescue centre could help you to get new skills and increase your chances of getting a job.

Check out **www.volunteeringireland.com** to read about a variety of opportunities.

You can also take up voluntary work while signing on. Under the Social Welfare Voluntary Work Option you can take up voluntary work in a community organisation and keep your jobseeker's allowance/benefit. To avail of this option you must be available to work and genuinely seeking work. Further information is available on **www.welfare.ie**.

I Don't Know What I Want To Be or Do

Choosing a College

When I was in 6th Year my guidance counsellor sat me down in his office and told me that he thought I was an aesthete. Seven years, an Undergraduate and a Master's degree in English Literature later, I finally worked out what that word means.

At seventeen I didn't know at all what I wanted to be or do; just what I didn't want to do. Throughout the year I went to various events, from the overwhelming overload of students and universities packed into the RDS for Higher Options, to speakers from different universities visiting, to various Open Days at different universities. For me the CAO part of my 6th Year was a meandering process, where I picked up certain courses out of the multitude, put them on my CAO form and then swapped them out for another later on.

Initially I took a fancy to Anthropology, then Psychology, English, French, Sociology.... I didn't finalise my choices in terms of ranking until the Change of Mind in June. For me that was a perfect opportunity to look at my options again with a clear post-Leaving Cert head and finalise my choices. I can't stress the importance of populating your CAO form if you're not too sure which exact courses you will end up getting – I really wasn't sure what I would get points-wise, and actually initially ended up with my fifth choice. Almost all of the five choices were for UCD.

Why did UCD appeal to me – someone from a village in Louth who knew no one studying there? Firstly, there was the place itself. I loved the feel of the campus when we took a tour on the Open Day – a little out from the city centre, it had more space to have its own atmosphere, and was much greener than the other universities I had visited. Secondly, relatively few people from my year were even considering going there – usually people prefer the opposite, but DCU was so full of people I'd spent the previous six years with it seemed more like an extension of Dundalk than Dublin. I found the UCD campus the perfect size – big enough so that you always meet new people, but yet small enough that from just walking to the library from the Arts Building you could bump into several of your friends. The sheer amount of on-campus activity due to such a large and diverse number of students appealed to me from the start.

In the CAO First Round I was offered Arts. There were several reasons I chose it, the main two were flexibility and choice. In first year I could pick classes from almost thirty different subjects. I especially liked the opportunity to try things you never had the chance to do in secondary school, such as Philosophy or Linguistics. Secondly, I found that the combinations of subjects you choose really form what you take from the degree – I did English, Psychology, and Linguistics in first year, and the latter two really informed my English major. A simple example of this at work would be my friend who studied French and Archaeology, who is now an archaeologist in France – the two subjects dovetailed perfectly for him.

A few weeks into the first semester I was marked up in my Leaving Certificate rechecks and was offered Single Honours English, and I gladly accepted the opportunity. It meant that from second year I would be taking almost all English classes. The best thing about Single Honours English was the class – there were twelve other students who were in the exact same position as me with the same interest in English. My favourite year was undoubtedly final year, where there were more than forty classes to choose from (the largest choice of any undergraduate degree in Ireland). In my case I took a module called 'Modern American Literature' in second year, and in third year there were eight classes on the subject to choose from; you really became well acquainted with every facet of literature, from pre-Shakespearean works to modern Irish Novels from the previous year.

Another one of the reasons I chose my course was the option of studying abroad. Looking back it was an amazing opportunity – I could choose from any number of top universities across Europe and the globe, at the same time transforming my degree into an International Bachelor of Arts, giving my CV an altogether more cultured look. I had to decide between studying in the Sorbonne University Paris, or the University of San Jose, California. In the end I opted for Paris due to the language dimension, as well as chance to study at one of the most famous universities in the world – I experienced great lecturers, but also an entirely different education system. The skills and insight I picked up during my Erasmus experience have really stood to me ever since.

Advice for Sixth Years

My advice for Sixth Years is definitely to take advantage of the increased opportunities available to you.

- It may sound obvious, but make sure to go to Open Days or at least get a tour of the campuses you are interested in – it's vital to get a feel for the place you could end up spending four years in, or more! You may find a course you really like but if you don't enjoy where you're studying it that makes things a lot harder, and vice-versa.

- Ask any people currently studying at the university whether they like their course and whether they like the university itself. This can give you good insights that you may not find in a prospectus.

- You are looking at college options in a time where you have so much more information directly accessible to you than any other generation – make use of it! All universities have more detailed course information, videos, and content online via their websites and social media than ever before. It's also a great opportunity to have any questions you might have answered directly by university staff themselves at any point on your CAO journey.

Matthew

May

- You may use the CAO Change of Mind facility between 5 May and 5.15 p.m. on 1 July to make changes to your Level 8 and Level 7/6 course choices, but not for introducing restricted courses which you have not already listed. The service is free of charge.
- 1 May is the final date a Leaving Certificate student may make an initial application to the CAO for a college place in the coming academic year. The online application fee is €50 at this stage.
- Before the end of May all CAO applicants will be sent a Statement of Application Record as a final acknowledgment and to enable them to verify that all information has been recorded accurately. You will also receive a Change of Mind Form. You may make as many changes as you wish online or by paper. If the forms do not arrive by 1 June, you must contact the CAO immediately.
- Given the proximity of the Leaving Certificate examinations it would be a good idea to leave final consideration of any course choices until you are finished in the third week in June, unless you have already come to a final decision on the order of the courses you wish to apply for.
- UCAS – if you received all your universities/college decisions by 31 March you must reply to any offers in early May or they will be declined. See the UCAS website for more information. If you applied by the January deadline and you're still waiting, all the universities will decide whether they're making an offer at this point. If you don't receive any offers those choices are automatically made unsuccessful.
- Open Days, interviews and enrolment days take place in many colleges this month, including Ballsbridge CFE, Killester CFE, Ormonde CFE, Bray Institute of Further Education and Open Training College, Dublin.
- The SUSI application process opens in early May. Check the SUSI website and social media channels closer to the time for updates on the actual date.
- The SUSI application process opens in early May. Check the SUSI website and social media channels closer to the time for updates on the actual date.

The Final Countdown

Getting Ready for the Leaving Certificate

For most Leaving Certificate students your school days are now almost over and the stark reality of sitting English Paper 1 at 9.30 a.m. in a month's time is staring you in the face. If you manage your time properly you can improve greatly on your potential grade performance over the next few weeks. You should undertake to do some structured study every day, in blocks of no more than three hours. Just don't wait for someone to tell you what to do – you have to make your own luck from now on.

Over the next few weeks before the exams you have sufficient time, if used effectively, to:

- Pull all that you have learned over the past two years together.
- Practise presenting your knowledge in the most exam-friendly manner.
- Strengthen your weak spots.

It's possible to do this while living a balanced lifestyle, exercising, eating well and giving yourself the occasional treat to keep yourself going. And remember – you also need to sleep!

Exam Tips

 ## Use Stress Effectively to Redouble Your Motivation

The best way to rid yourself of the stress you are feeling right now is to get stuck into a solid study routine. Sitting around worrying about how you are going to make it through the exams will get you nowhere. Facebook friends will still be there after the exams are long over, so stay away from the computer and turn off your phone. Use the stress you are feeling to help you maintain your focus over the coming weeks.

If exam stress does become a real problem for you consult your family doctor, who will be able to help you deal effectively with it.

2. Plan Your Last Five Weeks of Study

Allowing for gaps between exams after the first week's papers are completed, you can clock up over **200 hours** of high quality revision before you sit the last paper.

Print out your exam timetable from **www.examinations.ie** website and, working backwards from your last paper, map out exactly when you are going to tackle every single question on your study plan. If you don't have a plan, draft one right now, using the past papers as a guide. You may be surprised to realise that you can still cover the vast majority of your course curriculum if you punch in a solid day's work each day.

Your study will be most effective if:

1. You are writing short summaries of key points on each question onto mind maps that you can review the evening before the paper itself.

2. You practise writing out answers to past questions within the timeframes you will have on the day of the exam itself.

3. You do no more than three hours across four questions before taking a break for at least an hour.

4. You keep yourself hydrated with water and avoid sugar highs; failure to do this will play havoc with your capacity to concentrate.

5. You do not get panicked into concentrating all your efforts into an area of identified weakness, while letting other areas slide. If you feel unsure of your capacity to answer a particular question, ask your teacher for an hour of their time. Most will be more than happy to help out.

Don't get dehydrated

Top Tip! Combine the study tips above with a balanced approach to nutrition, exercise, sleep and relaxation over the coming weeks, so that you will be in the best shape possible when the day of the exam arrives.

3 Teacher Knows Best

Don't abandon the support available from your teachers in the final few weeks of school. They have huge experience of preparing students for exams as well as having taken a few in their own time.

Don't be tempted to seek last minute grinds if you run into trouble with a topic or subject. Go into school and ask your teacher to clarify the topic for you. If you still don't understand it sufficiently to feel confident to answer a question on the topic say so. The teacher won't be annoyed but will respect you for your honesty and will persevere until you overcome your difficulty. Such challenges are what motivated us to become teachers in the first place. Helping students to overcome mental blocks gives most teachers an enormous sense of professional satisfaction.

If your teachers are offering either formal or informal classes once 6th year teaching terminates in late May, tap into their expertise. There are also very good sources of online content available.

 ### 4 The Marking Schemes

To succeed, just reorganise what you already know – it's the key to high grades. Doing well in examinations is fifty per cent technique and fifty per cent knowledge of your subject matter. You have absorbed many times more information over the past two years than you could ever present in your Leaving Certificate. So, the next five weeks should be about fine-tuning your answers, in line with the marking schemes, published by the State Examinations Commission on www.examinations.ie.

The marking schemes are a vital resource for you. They will show you exactly what the teachers correcting your paper will be looking for when they start working on your exam scripts on a hot afternoon in July. Two students with the same amount of information on a topic may get radically different grades, depending on how they present the knowledge through their written answers.

⑤ Key Points

When you sit down to read your paper on the day of the exam remember that four or five key points are all that you will need in order to answer any question comprehensively. Once you write down these points, you will find that the information all starts to fall into place in your mind. So when you are studying try to reduce your recall triggers to no more than a handful of points or key words on any topic.

⑥ Your Support Network

Your parents and other family members are your most valuable supports. The best support a parent can give you at this stage is to listen and they may also be able to help you in practical ways. It may be as simple as your parent being at home more often to ensure a calm, quiet atmosphere in which you can study or keeping you well fed as your exams approach. Whatever it is don't be afraid to ask for their help.

⑦ Don't Get Distracted

Avoid any actions or activities that will knock you off course on the final lap. You must remember that performance on the day of the examination is determined by physical, psychological and emotional well being, as well as by how well prepared you are in the subject material. Physical well being is determined by a healthy well-balanced diet and exercise and, as always, you need to avoid alcohol and drugs.

Your Career Journey – Third Level

Most students become restless and excited as they contemplate the end of the school year and the three months of freedom ahead but among 6th Years the atmosphere is totally different. A deadly, almost sacred, silence descends on the year group as the first week of June approaches. They unconsciously huddle together to provide each other with emotional support. They are sharply aware that they are standing at the departure gate of their school life and they are about to leave forever the only world they have ever known.

Inevitably the moment arrives when it is time to shake hands with your teachers and walk out that gate for the last time as a second level student. You arrive home later that evening somewhat stranded in no-man's land, but with hopes and dreams of securing an apprenticeship, a job, a college place, or some other as yet unrealised aspiration, as a next step on your career journey of life with only the last hurdle of the Leaving Certificate looming across your pathway. But how do you turn those hopes and dreams into reality?

Motivation is a key component in your exam preparation to help you achieve these hopes and dreams. If you think ahead and visualise yourself in college or a job or starting an apprenticeship it will help you to focus on your study in the weeks ahead.

Below, Dr John McGinnity, Admissions Officer/ Assistant Registrar at NUI Maynooth has listed Ten Tips to help you make the most of your transition from school to third level.

Ten Tips for Third Level

The Leaving Certificate year is undoubtedly a very significant time in the life of a young adult. Whether you are currently in senior cycle in school preparing for the Leaving Certificate examinations and making your CAO choices or you have already received the offer of a place in college, you will quickly move to focus on the next step on your educational journey – going to college. For the unsuspecting student it can be quite overwhelming. However, with a little thought and forward planning, the transition to third level can be an exciting and refreshing process.

From my experience of working with new students over many years, the following tips will guide you towards making your further education a stimulating experience:

1. **Be proactive in your learning – take personal responsibility for your study:** The timetable within third level education differs greatly from anything experienced at second level. Lectures are usually fifty minutes and will therefore

require attention and a level of concentration at a higher level than you have experienced in a classroom setting. Free time within the schedule should be seen as an opportunity for research and study. This will require personal planning and a balance between socialising with friends and going to the library to revise the lecture.

Top Tip! Two fundamental facts are worth noting for the duration of your college studies – on average you should spend two hours of personal study time for each contact hour in lectures; and the sooner you revise your notes after lectures the more you will be able to fill in any gaps you have and the more of the learning will stay with you.

In many instances there are small group tutorials which will meet subsequent to the lecture to explore the topic further and provide a greater opportunity for your questions to be addressed. The tutorials provide an important support to the material covered in the lectures.

2 **Study differently:** Study at third level introduces students to the arena of analysis and critical debate. This requires not only a deep interest in one's subject area but also a willingness to read widely, based on guidelines proposed in lectures and tutorials. Much of the material on your course will be available in advance on an online student portal, such as 'Moodle' or 'Blackboard', which will provide lecturer notes and comments on preparing for the lecture. Your lecturer will use these notes and reading as a basis for his/her lecture.

Attendance at lectures and tutorials is highly correlated with good results; while there is a temptation to miss lectures as attendance may not be monitored it is a false illusion as you will very quickly fall behind in your studies.

3 **Get to know the language of college – a new lexicon:** The academic year is usually taught over two semesters of varying duration but generally they fall into a fifteen week schedule which includes lectures, tutorials, laboratories, continuous assessment and final examinations.

Each subject is divided into different modules, with each module having a credit value (normally 5 credits).

A module is a sub-section of a subject that is taught and assessed within each semester. The good thing is that having passed the module you will not be examined in that material again as you will move on to new learning and modules in the next semester.

A total year of study will have a value of 60 European Credit and Accumulation System (ECTS) credits. When you have attained 180 credits (3-year programme) or 240 (4-year programme) credits you will receive your degree award at a conferring ceremony.

At the beginning of the semester there may be an opportunity to choose from a range of subjects (or electives within subjects). Try to attend the lectures of all the possible subjects and not wait until three or four weeks have passed before you make your choice as that means that you will have missed important material after you have switched electives.

4 **Get to know where the goalposts are!** In third level your results are aggregated to give you an overall percentage (or grade point average) at the end of each year and in your final degree result, unlike in the Leaving Certificate whereby each subject just gets a grade.

Entry to postgraduate studies is competitive, with many requiring a Second Class Honour, First Division, so it is important to start studying from the beginning to achieve the highest result you can. Often there is a contribution from earlier years in your degree towards your final grade, so start your pattern of study from the early stages of your undergraduate education. Deadlines are important – at second level missing an essay or project deadline may not carry the same penalty as it does at third level. Failing departmental deadlines could have quite an adverse effect on the overall year's work. There will also be deadlines for choosing elective courses – it is important to be aware of these as some may be filled on a 'first-come, first-served' basis.

- 70% or more is a First Class Honours
- 60–69% is a Second Class Honour, First Division
- 50–59% is a Second Class Honour, Second Division
- 40% is the Pass grade
- In some instances a Third Class Honour is given 45-49%.

5 **Talk to your lecturers:** Within third level students have an opportunity to make contact with academic staff to seek direction and advice but it tends to be on a different level to that experienced within a school setting. In second level pupils are well known to their teachers, often on a first name basis; many students may find it a little disconcerting to no longer have that facility available to them. Initially, being part of a class of 200 students is a completely different experience to sitting in a classroom with twenty-five students.

Lecturers will have posted weekly student visiting times on their doors when you can drop-in for advice. Have the confidence to ask them questions on a one-to-one basis during their office hours – it is a great way to learn more about the subject beyond the classroom. Your lecturer will want you to succeed and will be delighted that you are taking an interest in their subject.

6 **Join a few clubs and societies:** Colleges find that students who join clubs and societies within the first few weeks in third level find it a lot easier to settle in and make friends. Clubs refer to sports clubs, e.g. football or basketball, whereas societies would include groups such as drama or debating. Most clubs and societies are run by students for students.

Outside of the halls of study and the world of lectures, it is essential to meet up with other like-minded (and not so like-minded!) students who may share the same interests as you do. This will expand your social circle and provide an opportunity for you to meet students from other courses across the college.

Being active in a club or society will add to your CV and give you something to talk about at interviews, either for summer jobs or after you finish. But ensure it is all in balance – too much time in clubs and societies will have an adverse effect on your results.

7 **Ask for help if you find yourself in difficulty:** It is essential to seek help and advice as early as possible should you find yourself out of your depth, whatever the problem. Most higher education institutions operate an open door policy whereby students are free to pop in for a chat and advice if they are uncertain or feeling a little lost. This may be in the academic department in which you are registered or to a central office which manages student administration or student services. Usually issues are quickly resolved but not seeking advice in time could be detrimental to successfully completing this important first year of study.

Many institutions have mathematics and writing support centres where you will have a chance to refine your skills in a supportive environment, working with students who have already taken those courses in previous years. Numerous students before you will have encountered the same issues and the college staff will be able to guide you to help you through them. Academic writing requires you to know how to reference work that you have read and this is a skill which you will refine within your academic studies. Failure to reference material properly could mean that you will be deemed to have plagiarised the work of others which isn't acceptable in the college environment.

8 **Manage your budget:** Money management is increasingly problematic for students at third level due to the cost of student registration charges and living expenses with part- time work difficult to find – thus advance planning is crucial.

As a rule of thumb part-time work of more than ten hours per week can diminish your academic attainment. It will have a positive effect on your CV and gives you an insight into the world of work which will have benefits in the long run. Have a realistic expectation of what costs may be involved such as registration, travel expenses, books etc. and try to not run up too much unnecessary debt. Some banks will be able to assist through the provision of student loans.

9 Start the accommodation search early: In recent times the cost of accommodation has increased and it is important to start your search as early as possible. As usual the best bargains are always for those who begin before time.

You will find that different types of accommodation may suit you as you go through your undergraduate years and you become more knowledgeable about what you require. Sharing a house with other students and agreeing the distribution of workload and cooking can really be a great learning experience for life!

10 **Enjoy and have fun:** Your college years are to be enjoyed not endured! It is a fantastic opportunity to broaden horizons, make new friends and explore some of the many opportunities that will come your way. You may consider taking an international year abroad with support from the college or it may simply be that you get immense enjoyment from taking up a sport or joining a society that you never had the opportunity to experience before – the possibilities are endless.

A third level education is a transformative experience – rewarding to you in your personal development as well as giving rise to a higher salary based on your studies. More and more education is a life long journey where you will be studying and attaining new knowledge and skills throughout your life – it is all worth it!

Dr John McGinnity
Admissions Officer/Assistant Registrar
NUI Maynooth

Your Career Journey – The Defence Forces

Third level universities or further education colleges are not by any means the only options available to you after you leave school. As you prepare for your exams in June some of you may be hoping to go in a completely new direction after the Leaving Certificate results in August.

SPOTLIGHT ON IRISH DEFENCE FORCES

Formed in 1922, the Defence Forces offers numerous and diverse fields of employment – infantry soldier, air traffic controller, IT specialist, combat medic, ship's captain, weapons' specialist, military pilot – to name just a few. It is a demanding career, involving large amounts of time away from home – either on exercise in Ireland and Europe or on an operational deployment overseas with the United Nations (UN), European Union (EU) or NATO.

Role of the Defence Forces

The primary role of the Defence Forces, Óglaigh na hÉireann, is to provide for the military defence of the neutral, sovereign State of Ireland. It also protects the citizens and resources of the State and some of the most vulnerable people in the most hostile regions of the world. For example Ireland's elite Special Forces unit, the Army Ranger Wing (ARW), remains on standby 24 hours a day to deal with crisis situations at home (e.g. hostage or hijack situation) or on UN-approved operations abroad.

Below are some examples of the various roles of the three Services of the Irish Defence Forces:

1   **The Army** secures the maximum-security Portlaoise Prison, the Central Bank, Government Buildings and Áras an Uachtaráin, operates cash-in-transit and high security prisoner escorts operations with the Gardaí and also deals with Explosive Ordnance Disposal (EOD)

call-outs. The Defence Forces Training Centre (DFTC) is located in The Curragh Camp in County Kildare.

2   **The Naval Service** is primarily responsible for maritime defence and fishery protection but it also contributes to the State's law enforcement, search and rescue and emergency response capability. For example, the naval diving section is the State's principal technical dive response asset. The Naval Service patrols Ireland's 220 million maritime acres and together with An Garda Síochána and the Revenue Commissioners is a member of the Narcotics Joint Task Force. Its base and headquarters are located in Haulbowline County Cork.

3   **The Air Corps** provides airspace policing during VIP visits and supports state agencies such as the HSE with air ambulance missions and assists with forest fires, coastguard/Gardaí operations. It has regular maritime patrols to back-up the Naval Service and supports the Army with military air transport for troops. Its base and headquarters are at Casement Aerodrome in Baldonnel, County Dublin.

Joining the Defence Forces

Working for the Defence Forces will mean experiencing a new lifestyle as you are trained to undertake operations that are demanding, and possibly life threatening, either at home or overseas. There are many career opportunities, with ongoing training and education available in areas such as military skills

training, adventure training, weapon handling, driving, communications and trade courses. The Defence Forces also provides external accreditation of career training and education up to ordinary degree and master's degree level, in addition to providing access to certain external courses.

How Do You Join?

There are three entry levels for joining the Defence Forces:

- A Cadet
- A Recruit
- An Apprentice

CADETSHIPS

Officers are the managers, decision-makers and leaders of the Defence Forces and the cadet competition is held annually for the Army, Navy and Air Corps. Cadets receive a salary from the day they are enlisted and begin training.

The candidates must satisfy minimum educational entry requirements and undergo psychometric tests, a fitness test and group assessment. If successful to this point they will also complete an interview and a medical exam.

1   Army cadets engage in fifteen months training in the Military College, Curragh Camp, covering many fields of study, before taking up operational appointments as army officers.

2   Air Corps cadets engage in approximately thirty-six months of training: seven

months are spent in the Military College, Curragh Camp for basic military skills and the remainder in the Air Corps College, Baldonnel Aerodrome, where they study to become military aviators.

3   Naval Service cadets engage in approximately two years training. The first three months are spent in The Cadet School, Military College, County Kildare, learning basic military skills. The remainder of their Cadetship is spent in the Naval Base Haulbowline, on board naval vessels at sea, and in the National Maritime College of Ireland. At the end of the second year and on completion of exams, cadets will be qualified to carry out the duties of an Ensign.

RECRUITS

The enlisted ranks account for the vast majority of personnel in the Irish Defence Forces. No formal education qualifications are required for joining but there is an interview and psychometric testing process.

Recruits are paid from the day that they join the Defence Forces and they all have one thing in common – seventeen weeks of intense training. All recruits become skilled in foot and arms drill, rifle marksmanship, field craft and military tactics.

APPRENTICES

Aircraft Technicians maintain the Air Corps' modern fleet of aircraft. A candidate must have obtained the minimum educational requirements in the Irish Leaving Certificate/National Equivalent. Trainee technicians are paid from the day that they join the Defence Forces.

On successful completion of a four-month basic military training course, an apprentice aircraft technician will commence a three-year Level 7 degree course in the Technical Training School of the Air Corps College at Casement Aerodrome. A further three months of military training completes the programme.

For more information on the various requirements and criteria for joining the Defence Forces, and also on rates of pay and how to apply, see www.military.ie/careers

Psychology & the PLC Route

I completed my Leaving Certificate before my seventeenth birthday and I think I was probably a bit overwhelmed at the prospect of going directly onto a university or institute of technology programme at that stage. I had been working with my guidance counsellor and examining all of the course options on offer around Ireland, at all the different levels on the Qualifax website. I was drawn towards psychology, but still wasn't ready to make a four-year commitment to that particular career path. I wasn't sure if I wanted to become a psychologist.

Finding a Course

One of the courses that my research identified was a one-year psychology programme offered by Senior College Dun Laoghaire. It's now the Blackrock Further Education Institute. I had not been aware up to that moment of the wide range of one and two year programmes offered by Post Leaving Certificate colleges throughout the country. I went onto their website to find out more about the college and decided to attend one of their Open Days to explore the course more fully and to talk to the lecturing staff.

After this visit I very quickly came to the conclusion that the psychology course was perfect for me. I could get a taste for psychology before I had to decide to commit full-time to a degree course.

In August of that year the results day came around. I was really nervous but did very well. The following Monday morning the letter from the CAO arrived offering me a place in the Applied Psychology course in the Institute of Art Design and Technology (IADT). While I was thrilled with the offer from the CAO I had already decided to seek a deferral of my offer for one year and to accept the PLC place.

Getting Started

The modules of Criminology and Behavioural Studies are what interested me in this course, but what also caught my attention the most were the links to other third level courses. Although I had already secured my place in IADT, it was great to have the opportunity to apply to Napier University in Edinburgh. The College also has links to IADT and that was particularly useful for some of my friends on the course who did not get enough points to get into their course directly through the CAO application process.

Result

My overall experience of the Applied Psychology course was fantastic. I learned so much and discovered where my interests really lay. Although I wasn't very interested in Child Development before I started the programme, it turned out to be one of my favourite subjects.

The workload was heavy but it prepared me for my further studies in IADT. I gained knowledge on how to write essays and organise my workload. The teachers were always helpful and answered any questions I had.

Clara

I would highly recommend the PLC route to anyone even slightly interested in any of the courses on offer in colleges throughout the country. It's a great way to try new things and to test if a certain pathway is right for you before you spend a fortune on the wrong choice!

10 June

JUNE FOCUS

- The Leaving Certificate Exams begin on the first week of June.
- CAO applicants under-23 years of age who have applied for one or more of the five undergraduate medical degrees and who sat the HPAT undergraduate medical entry aptitude test in March will receive their results on the first Monday after the end of the last written Leaving Certificate.
- All students can make amendments to their CAO applications until 1 July. Students whose HPAT result is below the threshold where an offer of a medical place would seem possible, even with a very high Leaving Cert performance, may choose to drop the medical courses from their application list at this point and to select other courses.
- UCAS – by the end of the first week in June candidates must have replied to offers received in the first week of May. The final date for UCAS applications is the end of June.
- Check out summer Open Days and Enrolment Days in Ballsbridge CFE, Open Training College, NUI Maynooth and Dublin Business School.

CAO Change of Mind

For the vast majority of 6th Years nothing other than your Leaving Certificate performance matters until after the end of the third week of June. That is why the CAO allows you at least ten days after the final written paper before it closes down the course choices aspect of your application.

From the perspective of making the most appropriate course choices the week following the completion of your exams is in fact the most important one in the entire year. Virtually every current Leaving Certificate applicant makes an amendment to course choices in May/June.

Over 6,000 students don't even list any of their course choices until this stage of the application process. The rules of the CAO allow for this, although they discourage you from leaving your course choices this late. For the thousands of students who have as yet to select any course now is your last chance to act before the 1 July deadline. Otherwise you will have gifted the CAO your application fee and be out of the application process for the current year.

Student Profile...

Name: **Andrea**

Degree: I've just completed a Bachelor of Arts in Advertising and Marketing Communications in the Institute of Technology Tallaght.

CAO Application: I had absolutely no idea what I wanted to do. I felt that I was too young to decide what path I wanted to go down. Everyone in my year was choosing courses in UCD and DCU, and out of pressure I put them on my CAO too. My first choice was Journalism in DCU and second was Arts in UCD, but both of those courses offered nothing I was ever interested in. To be honest, I wanted to be with my friends.

Points: I didn't get the points for either of those courses and looking back now, that was probably the best thing that ever happened to me. I was at a place then where I had to think about me – my abilities and my interests.

Plan B: It was coming closer to September and I had to decide what to do. I began looking at Institutes of Technologies and their course content. I moved away from the pressure of going to a University. In school I had studied Business and it was one of my best subjects. Institutes of Technologies such as IT Tallaght and DIT offer brilliant business courses in Management and in Marketing and Management. I liked Business in school, but it's a lot different to studying those courses in college. So I decided the best thing to do was to do a PLC in something along those lines, to get a feel for it and to see if I was 100 per cent sure that's what I wanted to do, before committing myself to four years.

Course: I completed a one-year FETAC course in Business Administration and within that year I found a love for marketing communications.

2nd CAO Application: My second time around at the CAO I was a lot more careful with my choices. I spent hours upon hours on Qualifax, looking at courses, and researching Colleges. Advertising and Marketing Communications in ITT was my first choice.

Result: I am now an Account Executive in an advertising agency. I started work the week after my finals. I am so grateful to ITT and everything they did for me. The small class sizes meant that the lecturers really got to know all of the students, helped point us in the correct direction and got us in contact with people in the industry. We also got to know everyone in the class really well. I've now met friends for life. An original worry of mine was that I wanted to be with my friends but I had no idea of the friendships that were ahead.

Top Tip: What I would say to 6th Year students today is – don't worry about what other people are doing, what they are putting on their CAO, or what college they are attending, think about yourself and what's best for you. And I would highly recommend an Institute of Technology, in particular, Tallaght. The courses there are constructed to equip the students with necessary skills and preparation for the working world. I thank IT Tallaght for the position I am in now.

Best of luck to everyone; you all have such exciting times ahead!

Graduate Salaries

In a recent report published in early 2014 by Thomas Conefrey and Richard Smith of the Central Bank of Ireland there are two elements that are particularly relevant to all 6th Years who are now considering their CAO options.

1   The report states that the number of people employed in Ireland has grown by 58,000 since the beginning of the recession. Of that amount, 50,000 jobs have gone to graduates and graduate employment has continued to grow during the crisis.

This is a very significant point for all Leaving Certificate students to keep in mind, particularly any of you who may be thinking about trying to enter the labour market directly following your exams.

2   They also discovered that starting salaries have fallen across a wide range of faculties. For example:

- In 2012 graduates in the Arts, Humanities and Social Science received an average salary that was 19.1 per cent lower than the amount graduates demanded in 2007, falling from an average of €24,445 to €19,748.

- The weighted average salary for Agriculture and Science graduates fell by 15.4 per cent and 12.9 per cent, respectively.

- Commerce and Business Studies graduates' salaries experienced the smallest decline during the downturn. Graduates in 2012 received an average weighted salary of €23,860, a drop of only 5 per cent compared to 2007.
- Architecture graduates, with a low participation rate reflecting the collapse in the construction industry, were the most affected with a fall of 31 per cent in the weighted average salary between 2007 and 2012.
- Average salaries across the remaining faculties dropped by between 7.7 and 11 per cent.

Many of you may not want to bring prospective salary scales into consideration when you are selecting your third level course but it could be something to factor into your selection of options.

Reassessing Your Course Choices

Whether you realise it or not, on the Monday morning after your exams finish you will move into a totally new world reality that you will inhabit for the rest of your adult life. You will become a former school student and, other than to pick up your Leaving Certificate results in August and return to attend past-pupil events, you are no longer a member of the second level school system.

Now is the time to reassess the career decisions you have made so far this year and decide if you need to change your CAO application. We have all seen the movie where the officer says, 'Don't shoot until you see the whites of their eyes.' The point being that the closer the enemy troops are to your defensive position when you shoot, the more accurate will be your aim. The same applies to your CAO College choices.

When you made your initial course choices back in December or January, going to college was a distant prospect and you were probably buried in preparations for your Leaving Certificate or Post Leaving Certificate programme. Now that the examination season is drawing to a close your mind is free of all those pressures and anxieties. You now have at least a week to ten days to calmly finalise your list of course choices.

Look at your current CAO course choices and try to picture yourself on that Wednesday morning in mid-August as you nervously open your Leaving Certificate results and quickly calculate your points score:

Remember

Remember, if you wish to make any adjustment to either or both your lists, you must resubmit the entire list in the order you now want your choices to appear. If you only listed the extra course(s) you want to add, your original choices would disappear from your application.

- Did you get enough points for your first choice or will you have to settle for one of the courses further down your list?

- If you don't get your first Level 8 course choice, will you accept your Level 7/6 first choice instead and spend an extra year studying to secure your original Level 8 degree course?

- Are you sure that you researched all the CAO options thoroughly? Did you study the full course content of each year's lectures on the Qualifax website and also the employment and postgraduate opportunities for all the courses you have listed?

- Did you select up to twenty courses and list them in the order you actually want them, allowing for all possible results?

- Did you double-check if any of your course choices had been discontinued?

Top Tip!

Courses are discontinued all the time and colleges also add new courses to the CAO system, so it is always wise to review all the courses on offer on the CAO or Qualifax websites. There are dozens of new courses on offer in June every year that were not in existence when the CAO printed their handbook last summer.

- Did you explore each course fully? Did you enter your area of interest into the course search field on the Qualifax website and make sure you meet the entry requirements, i.e. through having taken the required subject, at the appropriate level, in your Leaving Certificate or equivalent examination?

- Before you finalised your choices did you discuss them with your parents and your guidance counsellor? If you contact your school now the guidance counsellor will probably be happy to meet with you or at least discuss your choices over the phone.
- Many of my own students make appointments to meet me in late June, before they depart from school at the end of May.

If there is any doubt in your mind as to the quality of your CAO application or the degree to which you have researched every choice you have listed, now is the time to fix this before you take a well-earned break. If you do it over the next few days you should have no regrets about the quality of your CAO application when you open your results in August.

Even if you were convinced that the course choice list you submitted on 1 February was your final one, you should still go through the review process outlined above. Make sure to list your changes a few days before the 5.15 p.m., 1 July deadline, so that you do not end up trying to submit your choices at the last moment.

Point to note

The price of failing to reassess your course choices can be a costly one. If you end up accepting a course that is not appropriate for you, because you don't like the course content, having neglected to check it on the Qualifax or college website, or you realise that you have selected a course you have no interest in, you will either drop out during the year or fail your exams.

If this happens and you decide to return to college the following year to study another course, you will have to pay the registration fee again, PLUS the course fee. Remember, the Department of Education and Skills (DES) will pay the college on your behalf only _once_ for every year of an approved course. If you end up repeating a year you have to pay the fees. This could cost you a further €4,000–€5,000, making a total cost for your repeat first year of at least €7,000–€8,000. For many families today, this is way beyond their resources, especially when you factor in the living and accommodation costs of attending college as well.

Student Profile...

Name: Michael

Degree: Creative Digital Media four-year

CAO Application: Since I was in 4th/5th Year in school, I've always wanted to go on to do something in media, whether it was television or radio, so after doing a lot of research and attending open days, I knew that the courses that most suited me it would be between IT Tallaght, DIT or NUI Maynooth.

Points: Doing the Leaving Cert was stressful enough but then worrying about having to get certain points for courses and then the possibility of the course going up in points was hugely daunting. When I received my results I realised that my ideal course was out of reach by forty or so points.

Plan B: It was in late August/early September that I decided that I was definitely not repeating the Leaving Cert to try to gain a few extra points, nor was I taking a year out, so I decided I needed to research PLCs and quickly.

Course: I applied and was quickly accepted to a Multimedia Course in Stillorgan College of Further Education, Dublin. This course was so broad in media that I got a lot of experience in Design, Audio, Video Production, Web Design, Digital Photography and Animation.

2nd CAO Application: It was then after completing the course and reapplying through the CAO, I realised that the Multimedia course had got me a lot more interested in other aspects of media than just television and radio. As well as this, I realised that the advantages of being in such a small class gave me an opportunity for any individual attention or help I needed, which only a smaller Institute could offer, as opposed to a larger College or University. These thoughts influenced my thinking when it came to deciding which CAO courses to apply for. With the exception of one or two options, my CAO form remained unchanged from the previous year, but this time IT Tallaght's Creative Digital Media course was top of my list, because of its small class sizes and the wide spectrum of modules within the course.

Result: I have now just completed 2nd year of the Creative Digital Media course and I couldn't have chosen a better course for myself. The experience I gained through doing the PLC has helped me hugely with my course work. The last two years have been fantastic and I have learned so much that I am looking forward to the next and final two years of the course.

Top Tip: Looking back now, I realise that when I was in 6th Year and deciding on college courses, I didn't even attempt to research any PLCs. I had the attitude, 'I'm not after spending six years in school to do a PLC', which in my eyes were a route to college for people who didn't do well in school. I can now see how much of a huge mistake that was and how immature I was. That one year course has been so beneficial and it helped me to grow and become more mature before entering IT Tallaght. I would recommend to everybody to look at PLCs as an entry route to college.

At the end of the day, it will only help you in your studies and make it easier for you as it has done for me.

CAO Change of Mind Q & A

The beauty of life is in its tendency to throw up surprises that can have a profound effect on the pathways we end up travelling. All we can do to ensure that we best utilise the opportunities that life unexpectedly presents us with is to be as well prepared as possible. Use the advice in the answers below to help you take the first step on that journey.

Q. 1 How do I go about listing the most suitable courses in the correct order?

A. Many students use their initial application in January as a holding exercise, simply to secure their route to a college place this coming September. Now that you have to submit a final definitive list of options, you have to ask yourself which course or courses will build on your current attributes, interests and aptitudes, and strengthen your capacity to successfully enter the labour market at the end of your third level studies.

Top Tip! Remember that the work you put in over the next few days will pay huge dividends when you turn on the computer and log onto the CAO website on the third Monday in August next to get your results.

Q. 2 Now that I know where to find information on all the courses, how do I apply it to myself?

A. Most of you will have been through this process with your school's guidance counsellor over the past year. But if you are still uncertain you should revisit the following steps:

1 Take the interest inventory on both the Qualifax and Careers Portal websites and see if they highlight any areas of particular interest to you.

2 Re-read the results of previous interest inventory or differential aptitude tests you have undertaken in the past two to three years.

3 Look at the results you have achieved in your individual school subjects

over the past few years, including in your Junior Certificate. Are you performing above your average in one or more specific subjects? These subjects may be the ones to pursue in any undergraduate course you choose to study next year.

4 Reflect on any work experience or part-time work you have undertaken. Did it suggest a particular occupation or career path for you to follow?

5 Reflect on the subjects you are taking in your Leaving Certificate examinations. Which ones did you enjoy studying most? Which ones did you most enjoy writing about in the exam hall over the past two weeks?

The answers to all of the above questions may help you to narrow your course choices down to a relatively small number of suitable options.

Remember

Remember, fifty per cent of all students take a postgraduate course immediately following their undergraduate studies. Their intention is to use it to secure employment on the first step of their respective career ladders. Now is not the time to be contemplating what that step, which may be up to five to six years away, may be. You can address this question in your final year in college, when your options will be much clearer than they are today.

Q. 3 Why do I need to get involved with the Change of Mind process if I am happy with the choices I made in January?

A. If you are comfortable with your initial choice of courses and the order in which you have listed them, all you need to do is to check the list of courses you have applied for against the latest published list of courses on offer from the CAO. Ensure that all these courses are still on offer and that there are no new courses that you might like to take into consideration. Also ensure that you still meet all the subject and level of subject entry requirements.

If you are uncertain concerning what these requirements might be, go to the subject choice module in the Qualifax website, where the entry requirements for all courses are outlined. If some of these choices are no longer open to you, you now need to remove them from your list of choices and add new options.

If, however, having reviewed your choices, you are happy with your current application, you need take no further action. You do not need to communicate in any way with the CAO.

Q. 4 Should I use the online Change of Mind option on the CAO website or return any changes I want to make by post?

A. You should most certainly use the online option. This will ensure that you only apply for courses that are currently on offer, as the online system will not accept a discontinued course or a wrong course code.

Q. 5 I have not applied to the CAO this year, but am now considering applying for a college place. Is it too late to do so?

A. It is too late to submit an application to the CAO, as the final deadline for those seeking a first year undergraduate place for the first time was 1 May.

If you are a second level or PLC student and you have not as yet applied for a CAO place this year you may be able to apply for an available/vacant place. Once the colleges know exactly how many applicants have applied for each course on offer after the 1 July deadline, they will seek applications for available/vacant places. These course places will be listed on the CAO website on the Tuesday following the first round of CAO offers in the third week of August. Any existing or new CAO applicant can apply for these courses.

EXTRA! EXTRA!

Getting Paid to Study in College

Like many 6th Years, when I thought about what I would be doing when I finished my Leaving Certificate, I had a general idea of an area I was interested in, which for me was Business/IT. Just before 6th Year I took part in a business class competition that was like 'The Apprentice'. We were challenged with creating a new marketing campaign for a DIY merchant. Both campaigns were then presented in front of the manager and he chose the winner and we split the prize money. It incorporated teamwork, creativity, presentation skills , and got me massively interested in Business/Commerce. However, when it came to selecting courses to put down on the CAO form, I struggled and practically had a different course preference every week.

Sure, I had a keen interest in the given area, but not enough to commit myself to just one course. The external 'pressures' were then applied from family and friends over what you should/could do and what you most certainly shouldn't do. It's completely normal for everyone to try and help you (you can add me to that list), but at times you get the feeling you can't make everyone happy. Although it was actually my mother who gave me the application form for the Lidl-sponsored degree in Retail Management from Dublin Business School (DBS), which is what I ended up choosing.

I applied and out of 1,300 applicants, was one of the lucky forty to be selected. The three-year program is split evenly between working for Lidl in-store and studying for my business degree in DBS. These two aspects of the programme give me the unique ability to use what I'm learning in college in a real life work environment.

Not following the CAO route into college was unheard of to me before I was introduced to this programme. But there are businesses out there willing to sponsor students through college.

I worked in a store close to my home in Galway, training as a manager for four months, before going up to study in DBS for the next four months. Throughout these months I remained on a salary, so Lidl is showing great faith and belief in me. It's a big confidence booster knowing you're working for a multinational that sees your potential and invests in it.

Choosing a Course

What persuaded me to choose this programme over Commerce (which I was offered by the CAO) was the truly unmatched work experience. For someone who had barely worked a day in my life, I suddenly had a steady job with an income and clear career progression in sight. The independence on offer at my age was crucial in my decision. Some of my friends still can't believe I'm being paid to go to college.

The Retail Management degree covers areas such as marketing, human resource management and IT. It's a great opportunity to meet the other people on the course as well. You get to know everybody and there's a really strong work ethic in the class so learning is made easy.

The best part for me is that the programme incorporates presentations into a lot of group work and within a few weeks it really becomes second nature to you. The ability to stand up in front of people and speak is a massive skill and a huge opportunity to impress Lidl Head Office. It's a bit like 'Dragon's Den' but you feel much more prepared.

The work blocks in-store are where you need to show your teamwork, flexibility and energy. Lidl have been brilliant in training me up in all areas. I'm a fairly reserved guy at the best of times but having to engage with employees and customers has allowed me to develop a confidence and I'm starting to feel comfortable in the role. Decisions need to be made constantly, and you have to be ready to solve any problems that may arise with customers or staff.

You gain a comprehensive understanding of the retail business. Lidl being very standardised worldwide, means you have a fairly good idea of how things work in other stores. You also gain a comprehensive understanding of the entire retail sector and could work anywhere afterwards.

Upon completion of the degree, Lidl can offer me a range of roles, in their Head Office or as a store manager, and it's up to me now to show them what I'm capable of. Alternatively, I can go on to further education or apply for jobs elsewhere. It's essentially a three-year interview.

If you're unsure of what you are going to do next I'd say be open-minded when you are selecting what to do. Accepting a college place offered through the CAO will be right for the majority of people. But there are other options and I would continually research these options and apply for anything that may interest you. If your interest is in commerce, then look out for businesses willing to invest in you and give you the work experience advantage over other courses. The same applies for whatever interests you have.

Padraig

Applicants to the Retail Management Degree Programme: Minimum entry requirements are five passes at Leaving Certificate Ordinary Level including a C3 in Ordinary Level Mathematics and a D3 in English or another language, plus an overall minimum of 250 points. For further details see www.lidl-degree.ie.

11 July

- The CAO Change of Mind facility closes on 1 July at 5.15 p.m. This is your final chance to amend your twenty course choices or order of preferences on your CAO application.
- CAO Deferrals: if you requested a deferral of your place last year, you will receive your course place offer again, any time after 4 July. These offers will be available on the CAO website. If you do not accept the place within the specified time – **one week** – your offer lapses and you cannot retrieve it.
- The first offers for Mature and Deferred Entry applicants start around 4 July. The CAO will make over 6,000 offers to mature applicants, i.e. those over twenty-three years of age, and to those applicants who accepted and deferred the place offered to them the previous year. Make sure you don't miss out on these offers because you are away on holiday.
- The deadline for applications to Student Universal Support Ireland (SUSI), the national awarding authority responsible for student grants, is 1 August.
- UCAS – 2 July is the last date to apply through Extra. Check the UCAS website for final decision dates for university offers made in June/July.
- The exceptional closing date for late applications on the CAO website is usually the third week of July. It is for students currently studying at a third level college who wish to drop out of their course and re-apply for a new list of choices through the CAO application process.
- Colleges such as the Open Training College Dublin continue to run interviews and Open Days throughout July. Consult the individual college websites for more information.

What is SUSI?

Student Universal Support Ireland (SUSI) assesses grant applications from students hoping to attend approved further or higher education courses. It operates under a very tight processing timeframe between May and October every year.

The online application system opens in early May and in the 2014/2015 academic year over 96,000 students applied for grants. Applications are made online and are subject to students delivering the support documentation required within the specified timeframe.

Common mistakes in applications include students:

- Providing incorrect Personal Public Service (PPS) numbers for themselves.
- Listing incorrect dates of birth for other parties on their applications, for example their parents.
- Applying without including a full set of year-end trading accounts and an acknowledgment from Revenue that tax returns have been filed. This causes a problem when the income to be assessed is from self-employment or farming. In this instance applicants need to ensure the relevant tax returns have been filed early so that they can send on the support documentation.

Top Tip! Visit the SUSI website (www.susi.ie) to use its new online 'grant eligibility reckoner' where you can quickly and easily self-assess whether or not you are entitled to a grant.

Who May Be Eligible For a Grant?

Students attending:

✓ Approved Post Leaving Certificate (PLC) courses in Ireland.

✓ Approved Undergraduate courses in Ireland, the EU, EEA or Switzerland.

✓ Approved Postgraduate courses in Ireland or Northern Ireland.

What Are They Eligible For?

Post Leaving Certificate courses in Ireland:

- Maintenance grant only

Undergraduate courses in Ireland:

- Maintenance grant
- Student contribution charge
- Tuition fees (in certain cases)
- Compulsory field trips (in certain cases)

Undergraduate courses in the EU, EEA or Switzerland:

- Maintenance grant only

Postgraduate courses in Ireland or Northern Ireland:

- Postgraduate fee contribution or postgraduate tuition fees
- Compulsory field trips (in certain cases)

What Does a Grant Cover?

- **Maintenance Grant:** this is a contribution towards the living costs of a student and is paid over nine monthly instalments during the academic year.
- **Student Contribution Charge:** this figure is set each year, e.g. for 2015/16 the student contribution charge is €3,000. If it applies to a course, the grant will cover 100 per cent or 50 per cent of this cost, depending on household income.
- **Tuition Fees:** if a student, or a course, is not covered under the Free Fees Schemes, the grant will cover tuition fees subject to eligibility criteria.
- **Field Trips:** the grant will cover eligible expenses for compulsory field trips.
- **Postgraduate Fee Contribution:** a contribution of €2,000 is made towards the cost of the student's tuition fees.

Key Eligibility Criteria

✓ **Residency:** applicants must be resident in Ireland or the EU, EEA or Switzerland for three of the last five years.

✓ **Nationality:** applicants must be an Irish, EU, EEA or Swiss National or have specific leave to remain in the State.

✓ **Previous Education:** if applicants have previously attended further or higher education courses, regardless of whether they received a grant, this will be taken into account when assessing their application to ensure that they meet the 'progression' criteria.

✓ **Back to Education Allowance (BTEA):** if applicants are in receipt of BTEA and are attending a PLC course they will not be eligible for funding. If they are attending a Higher Education course they may be eligible for the student contribution charge and tuition fees.

Top Tip! Students can use the 'online application tracker' to track the progress of their application and confirm that SUSI has received their documentation.

✓ **Income:** household income is assessed for the tax year and must fall between one of the specified thresholds in order to qualify for grant funding.

Visit www.susi.ie for more information

Taking a Gap Year

In the UK and elsewhere there has been a long tradition of taking a Gap Year after finishing second level education. In Ireland your Gap Year probably happened in Transition Year, where you learned a whole new basket of skills. But if you are still genuinely unsure what you want to do after you finish the Leaving Certificate, considering a Gap Year could be a good alternative.

The value you will get from your year out will be determined almost entirely by the quality of your research before you go. Undertaking the research itself will be of considerable benefit to you – sorting out your passport, visa requirements, travel insurance, vaccinations and so on. You will have to develop a wide range of organisational skills that you can subsequently outline on your CV and use in your studies/jobs when you eventually start them.

What Could You Do During a Gap Year?

You can choose between many options:

- You could take a one year Post Leaving Certificate course in an area that will add to your existing skills base, e.g. business, computer technology/programming, fashion/design and so on.

- You could seek a job, either in Ireland or abroad. This may, however, be difficult to organise because of your age and relatively low skill base. Even if you succeed in securing a paid job, you will not earn very much, but it will very quickly make you understand the value of money and how hard it is to accumulate!

- You could choose to travel, experiencing new cultures, languages and people. But be aware this option is expensive. If you hope to work while you travel taking an accredited Teaching English as a Foreign Language (TEFL) course could help you to find a job when you are abroad or you could try contacting local recruitment agencies before you go.

- You could work as a volunteer in a local organisation for a year. Volunteers work in practically every part of Irish society from the Irish Blood Transfusion Service to Dublin Zoo. There are thousands of organisations across Ireland looking for help. Virtual volunteering is also an option.

- You could offer your services to a charity organisation to work in less developed parts of the world. But be aware that as a Leaving Certificate student you may not have the skills required. It costs a considerable amount of money to maintain a Western European in these areas. Look at the intercultural learning website to find out more about available opportunities.

There are many organisations, mainly UK-based, that organise Gap Year volunteering and charity activities in South America, Africa, India and so on. They are very well organised and your health and safety will be protected.

These Gap Year projects are also very expensive and unless your parents are in the lucky position to be able to fund you, or you have excellent fund raising skills yourself, you may not be able to consider this option.

- You could offer to work as an *au pair* with a family in another country, preferably where you could learn or improve your foreign language skills. In doing so you will also come to understand their culture and see your own life in Ireland in an entirely different light.

Deferring Your College Place

If you do organise a sustainable Gap Year you would be well advised to secure a CAO or other college place offer first and defer it for a year. In this way you always have a college place to come back to.

If during your Gap Year your interests totally change, you are in no way committed to your deferred place. You can make an entirely new CAO or other college system application based on the grades you secured in the Leaving Certificate when you get back.

The CAO offers you then receive will usually take place as early as the first week of July in the case of a deferred place or in the CAO round one in mid-August.

Useful websites:

www.gapireland.org   www.usit.ie/volunteer

www.i-to-i.com   www.projects-abroad.eu

www.volunteer.ie   www.onlinetefl.com

www.eilireland.org

Benefits of a Gap Year Abroad

If you travel overseas for your Gap Year it will contribute to your growth and development. This will happen naturally as you overcome new challenges and come to know yourself in a way you have never done before. You will also benefit hugely from the following new experiences:

- ✓ Living away from home.
- ✓ Looking after your daily needs – learning to cook and clean-up after yourself, doing your own washing and so on.
- ✓ Managing a budget.
- ✓ Building new relationships.
- ✓ Coming to understand new cultures and languages.
- ✓ Working as a member of a team.
- ✓ Doing manual work – this will give you a taste for the real world.

All these experiences will be extremely motivational when you return from your year out and find yourself working in a new job/apprenticeship or starting your studies. Hopefully you will come back full of energy and new insights, with a heightened sense of self-awareness.

Your Gap Year should have helped you to clarify your initial college choices and you will be in a far better position to start into your third level studies with an energy and purpose that will sustain you through the entire period. Alternatively, if you have decided to immediately search for a job, be sure to capture all of these rich new experiences in your CV as they will be impressive to any potential employer.

Top Tip!

Travelling in Africa with a student group, I found it extremely useful to sit down every evening for thirty minutes to diary that day's activities. On returning home this diary enabled me to relive the richness of the entire experience and to clearly see how it had changed my perceptions in so many ways. I would advise you to keep a diary of your Gap Year – using your laptop or a pen and paper!

Dangers of a Gap Year Abroad

Besides the benefits, there are also dangers associated with travelling in foreign countries, which you should be mindful of.

- Tropical diseases – if you are travelling to South Asia or South America you may require vaccines against a range of diseases including Hepatitis A/B, typhoid, cholera, malaria, diphtheria and rabies.

- Involvement in extreme sports – whether you want to try sky diving, bungee jumping from the Macau Tower, at 233 metres the highest jump in the world, skiing with the yaks in India, rolling downhill in a giant sphere in Cambodia or white-water rafting in South Korea, don't forget to consider your safety first. (I managed to avoid the temptation to impress my students by bungee jumping from the bridge joining Zambia to Zimbabwe at Victoria Falls.)

- Travelling in climates very different to our temperate one in Ireland can lead to significant burns and skin damage so don't forget to factor in the heat.

- Crime – be aware that the world can be a very dangerous place, unless you are careful about the situations you allow yourself to become involved in. Research areas online before you enter them and gather as much information as possible. Contact the local Irish embassy or police force if you are in any doubt about your safety while travelling.

- Social media – you or your property can be a very attractive proposition in less developed parts of the world, so exercise caution in situations you are unfamiliar with and don't pre-advertise your movements on social media accounts.

12 August

- The application process for SUSI closes in early August. Check the SUSI website and social media channels for updates on the specific closing date.
- The CAO commence Round Zero offers in the first week of August, offering approximately 2,000 places to certain categories who are not competing with current year Leaving Certificate students, e.g. graduate entry medicine applicants. Candidates have exactly one week to accept these offers.
- The State Examinations Commission delivers the Leaving Certificate results to over 700 schools nationwide in mid-August. Your results are also available online, at www.examinations.ie, from 12 noon on that date.
- The CAO release the Round One offers to candidates online at 6 a.m. the following Monday. Offer Notices are also sent to candidates by post and should arrive the same day. The minimum points required for entry to each course will also be available on the CAO website from 6 a.m. on that date. Candidates have **one week** to accept these offers.
- Just over two weeks after the exam results are delivered the CAO will post Round Two offer notices to applicants. The minimum points required for entry to each course will appear on the CAO website at 6 a.m. that day. Candidates have **one week** to accept these offers.
- Leaving Certificate students who wish to view a number of their examination scripts must complete their application form and return it to their school by the Tuesday after the exam results are issued.

Leaving Certificate Results Day

Calculating Your Points

If you are collecting your Leaving Certificate results from your school or checking online don't forget that you can calculate your points immediately with the points calculator app from Careers Portal.

Remember you can only use the results of your best six grades and not all colleges operate to the same points system.

- A growing number of colleges, particularly Institutes of Technology, offer some points for Grades A and B in foundation level Maths and Irish.
- At the other end of the spectrum, 25 bonus points for Higher-level Maths are offered by all colleges to those students who secure a minimum of a D3.

Consult your CAO handbook for details of all points variations.

These points will determine whether you will or will not be offered your registered course choices. Last year's points requirements should be a good guide regarding what the points will be this year. However, there is always some movement up and down, depending on the popularity of particular courses.

What Happens Next?

A few days after the results are issued the admissions officers of all the colleges will inform the CAO how many places to offer on each course. Several thousand CAO places have already been offered and accepted by now. This occurred as part of Round Zero, when the initial batch of CAO places were offered to:

- Students who had deferred a place from the previous year.
- Current year mature applicants.
- Students who secured a place reserved for those holding FETAC (now QQ1) Level 2 awards.
- Candidates for graduate entry medicine.

Colleges are like airlines in many ways, in that they will offer more places than they want acceptances for. They know that there will always be those who, for a variety of reasons, will not take up a place offered.

Sometimes, as with airlines, the colleges get it wrong and find themselves with more first round acceptances than they anticipated. Obviously in those circumstances they must honour their commitment and hope that some students change their mind, either before registration or early in first year.

Your CAO Offer

At 6 a.m. on the Monday following the exam results, the CAO will place all first round offers live on its website. Each one of you who applied to the CAO this year has an individual application number so you can access your own CAO file.

The CAO will also post out all offers to every applicant. These offers will arrive at each applicant's home on Tuesday morning.

In your personal CAO file, you may find one, two, or no offers. Hopefully, you are one of the fortunate ones receiving your first choice courses and you are now looking forward to life as a third level student.

Two offers are made when you have met the full entry requirements and points requirement for a course on both your Level 8 and Level 7/6 lists of course choices. If you have, you can now decide which of the two courses on offer best serves your long-term goals.

You may not have received any offer today, due to a variety of reasons, and are now considering other options for the coming academic year.

If you did receive an offer you will have **one week** to accept or decide to ignore the offer of a place(s).

Places can be accepted online or by post.

✓ If you're one of the small number of applicants who choose to post your acceptance, do so at least a day before the deadline and get a certificate of posting from your post office to ensure that it arrives safely. These certificates are printed on the inside back cover of the CAO handbook.

✓ If you are accepting online, using your access code and your password, you MUST print off a receipt of your acceptance before ending your online session with the CAO. Once you have access to an online computer anywhere in the world, this process takes a matter of minutes. It should be completed well before the cut-off date for acceptance of Round One offers by 5.15 p.m. on the Monday.

✓ If you do not accept your place by this deadline, the place will go back into the system for the second round offers.

Q & A – Your First Round CAO Offer

Q. I didn't get offered my first CAO choice but was offered one of my lower choices. What should I do now?

A. Having received an offer today, your first decision must be whether to accept it or not. You cannot assume that the points for your higher choice preferences will decrease in later rounds, as only a small number of places are offered after Round One, so do not rely on receiving any further offers.

If you do accept this offer your name will remain in contention for any courses higher up on your final two lists of CAO choices. This way you not only have the assurance of a third level place if you do not get any further offers, but your name remains in the running for a place on any of your preferred courses, should the points come down in later offer rounds.

If a place becomes available, whether you have accepted the first offer or not is irrelevant. You will simply have any registration fees you paid to the first college transferred to the second one at no extra cost.

Top Tip!

If you defer you must remember to reapply to the CAO next year, listing just that one course in your CAO application. If you list more than the deferred course, you are then back in open competition with next year's applicants.

Q. I would like to defer my CAO acceptance for a year. How do I do that?

A. If you want to defer your course place you must immediately contact the admissions office of the college in question and request permission to defer until next year, outlining your reasons. You do not need to contact the CAO as the college will do that on your behalf. The most likely scenario is that the college will allow you to defer.

Q. I got more points than I needed for my course, but I didn't get offered a place today. Why is that?

A. An offer of a place on any course is determined by three factors:

1 The college's own minimum entry requirement

2 The specific course subject entry requirement

3 The points score of the applicant.

These are all available to review on the Qualifax website. If you have the points, you are lacking one of the minimum entry requirements for that course. It may simply be that you have passed a minimum entry subject, but you needed a higher grade in it.

Another reason for not receiving an offer may be that you have failed to register a language exemption with the appropriate authority, e.g. the National university of Ireland (NUI).

You can gain entry to this course next year, by e.g. repeating the problem subject and second time around hopefully meeting whichever minimum entry requirement you are currently lacking or by contacting the NUI about that language exemption. You can carry this year's points forward and apply again for the course. But your result in next year's exam cannot be added to increase your points score overall, as you can only present the points secured in one sitting of the Leaving Certificate.

Q. I received an offer of one of my lower choices but I don't know anything about it. Should I accept it anyway?

A. Go to the Qualifax website and you will find the full details of the course you have been offered. Study them very carefully before you make any further decisions.

   If you have time visit the college itself and talk to a member of staff in the admissions office or in the faculty offering you the course place.

   If, having done that, you feel that this course will help you to develop your career interests, go online and accept your place. If on the other hand you feel that it really is not for you, let the offer lapse, as you will probably not see the course through to graduation.

Q. I do not wish to accept the offer that I have just received from the CAO. Do I need to do anything?

A. In your situation you need take no further action. Your name will remain on the waiting list for any course(s) higher up your order of preference, than the one currently offered to you. But be aware there is no certainty that you will receive a further offer.

Q. I didn't get a CAO offer. Do I have any options at all?

A. Yes, you do. You may still receive an offer of a place in Round Two. You can also check out the extensive list of available places that is updated daily on the CAO website. Places will become available if the original list of qualified applicants to the CAO is exhausted or if a college has offered a new course since 1 July.

Check that you meet all the minimum entry requirements on the course first. If you do, you may secure an offer of one of these places by simply amending your list on the CAO website and placing the course you are interested in on the top of your CAO list of choices.

If none of the available places courses interest you, you may consider the option of a Post Leaving Certificate (PLC) course. You could apply again to the CAO next year, presenting the result of your PLC course as your method of entry. In some cases a small number of places may still be available in the current academic year.

Q. I have been offered a place on a course, but cannot afford to accept it unless I qualify for a grant. Where can I find out if I qualify or not?

A. The maintenance grant is the main source of financial help available for students in full-time Post Leaving Certificate Courses (PLCs) and full-time higher education undergraduate courses offered through the CAO. Support is available to eligible students in most colleges in Ireland as well as eligible Irish students in many colleges in Northern Ireland, the UK and other EU States.

Family and/or personal income is a key factor that will be assessed when you apply for a maintenance grant but there are also some other conditions. Log on to www.studentfinance. ie and see pages 119–122 to find out more about SUSI, the grants authority.

Q. Where can I get information on securing accommodation at or near the course I have been offered today?

A. Each college has a comprehensive student accommodation service operated by either the college authorities or the students' union, or by both in the case of large colleges.

Many students who receive a first round offer immediately go to the college to try to secure accommodation for the year ahead. It might be worth your while following their example as most of the quality accommodation is snapped up very quickly.

Q. Do I have to pay a fee when returning my acceptance to the CAO?

A. No payment is required when returning the acceptance of a place. The college will send out any bills for tuition fees and so on separately. All enquiries about such fees should be directed to the Fees Office of the college offering the place – not to the CAO. Students will have to pay these charges when they are registering in their new college.

Q. I have the published points for the course I want, but have not received an offer due to random selection. What can I do now?

A. You may choose to accept the course you have been offered and hope that the college will attempt to clear all those on random selection in Round Two offers. There is no way of knowing how many students are on the same points as you and are waiting to see if any places become available. The technical operation of random selection is clearly outlined in the CAO handbook available on its website.

Q. I feel my results in some subjects are not a fair reflection of my work. If I successfully appeal my grades how will that affect any CAO offers?

A. In mid-October the State Examinations Commission (SEC) will automatically notify the CAO, in the event of a successful appeal of any grade you received in your results. You will then be contacted about any new courses this upgrade entitles you to join. As this happens up to six weeks after courses start, some courses cannot offer you a place this year due to the size of the existing class group. Many colleges, however, give you the option of taking up the place immediately.

If you want to accept the new course place but cannot get in this year you can defer entry until next year and do something else in the meantime. Don't forget if you do this you have to apply to the CAO again by 1 February next year, listing the deferred course as the only course choice on your application form.

Disability and Options Beyond Secondary School

In the run up to your Leaving Certificate you don't think beyond the exams and you don't envision what college life will actually be like.

Going to third level is a big change and the more advance planning you can do the smoother the transition will be. While this is something all students have to manage, students with disabilities may have some additional factors to consider:

1 Students with mobility or sensory impairments may have to consider if they can access public transport to get to college or have to arrange an alternative, like Vantastic, a door-to-door, subsidised wheelchair-accessible transport service for the Dublin area. There is a huge demand for this type of service so it is worth contacting it and making arrangements well before the start of the academic year.

2 Accommodation could be another issue. Accommodation in or near universities and colleges is notoriously difficult to find once college starts and may require extensive searching.

3 Negotiating the college campus could be challenging for some students with disabilities. Once you've registered with the college, link in with the disability support service. It will carry out a needs assessment to ensure that your disability doesn't put you at an academic disadvantage. For those of you who have already disclosed your disability on the college application form or on the CAO Supplementary Information Form the college's disability support service will already have your contact information and will arrange to meet-up. Make sure you attend the meeting as the support service won't keep chasing you! If you didn't disclose that you have a disability on your CAO don't panic – you can do this any time.

You might feel you got on fine in secondary school with little or no disability support, but third level is a completely different learning experience. Not only will you have to get to grips with academic writing and getting your assignments in on time, but you've also got to deal with the additional impact of disability in a new learning environment. Getting disability related support such as assistive technology or a sign language interpreter from the start will help to ensure that the impact of your disability is dealt with and you can get on with the tough but enjoyable task of being a student.

4 Even if you receive a range of disability supports you still have to take responsibility for your own learning. If you don't hand in your assignments on time or attend lectures no one will come looking for you. Be aware that you could run the risk of failing the year and having to sit repeats at an additional financial cost.

Points to note

The disability-type supports that you might need are paid for through the fund for Students with Disabilities and it's available for students who are studying full-time, from a QQI (formerly FETAC) Level 5 to PhD level. The fund is not available if you are pursuing a QQI course lower than Level 5, if you are studying a part-time course or if you are attending a private college.

5 After years of the regimented system of secondary school the new-found freedom can be both liberating and daunting; you're in a new environment where the chances are you know no one. But remember the majority of freshers are in the same boat as you. Enjoy the experience because it's true what they say – college years really are the best years of your life!

Top Tip! The number of students with a disability moving from second to third level courses increases every year. According to a recent study published by Ahead Educational Press they currently represent 4.6% of the student population.

If you'd like more information about going to college you can contact AHEAD on 01 7164396 or lorraine.gallagher@ahead.ie

Reviewing Your Exam Scripts

If you feel that any grade you receive in your Leaving Certificate results is not a fair reflection of your work, you may apply to view the script. This free service offers all candidates the opportunity to see how the marking scheme has been applied to their work, and will help them to decide whether to appeal a result.

With the exception of external candidates, all applications to view papers should be made through your school. External candidates are students who studied for the exam outside a standard second-level school, i.e. at a grind school to repeat the year or on their own. These candidates should follow the instructions in the provisional statement of results they received directly from the State Examinations Commission (SEC).

The closing date for receipt of completed application forms in schools is the Tuesday of the week after the CAO Round One offers.

Your Scripts and the Marking Schemes

Marking schemes in all subjects will be published by the SEC on their own website in the days leading up to the viewing of scripts and will be provided to schools as well, to facilitate the process.

You will be able to see how the SEC marking schemes were applied for all the papers you may wish to examine. You also need to be familiar with previous marking schemes (see www.examinations.ie).

It is extremely useful if your own teacher/teachers are present when you are viewing the scripts as they can immediately spot where you have not been awarded marks that should have been given under the tenets of the marking scheme.

If your teacher/teachers do agree to turn-up they are doing it in their own time, out of their commitment to you, and won't be paid to do so.

Viewing Your Exam Papers

The viewing of scripts will take place in schools on Friday and Saturday over the last weekend of August – early September. You have to be there yourself to view the script. It is strictly forbidden to nominate someone to view a paper on your behalf.

The viewing sessions for the examinations are usually as follows:

✓ **Session 1:** Friday evening from 6.00 p.m. to 9.00 p.m.

✓ **Session 2:** Saturday morning from 9.00 a.m. to 12.00 noon.

✓ **Session 3:** Saturday afternoon from 2.00 p.m. to 5.00 p.m.

The Next Step

If you are unhappy with any of your grades following the viewing of the paper you should consult the Leaving Certificate Results Appeal Process booklet that accompanies your statement of provisional results. Follow the instructions carefully to ensure you lodge valid requests for appealing results. This information is also available in the candidates section on the State Examinations Commission (SEC) website.

What is the Deadline/Fee for Appeals?

All appeal applications must be with the SEC by 5 p.m. on the Wednesday following the viewing dates.

The fee per subject, refundable in the case of a successful appeal, is:

- Leaving Certificate Established   €40.00 per subject
- Leaving Certificate Applied   €15.50 per subject

What Are the Chances of an Upgrade?

On average approximately 18 per cent of appeals are successful.

Think about that figure for a moment. If you are five or ten points short of your target to secure your desired college place, appealing gives you a chance to make up this shortfall. Otherwise your only option is the hope that the points drop due to more places becoming available as students fail to register for a course that they accepted. With an appeal, given the pattern of recent years, you have almost a one in five chance of securing an upgrade.

Don't automatically appeal the paper in the subject you are disappointed in. View the scripts of every subject other than where you have secured an A1. Be strategic in deciding which subjects to appeal.

By viewing all your scripts you get to see the exact percentage grade that you secured in every subject you took in your Leaving Certificate. After the viewing process you therefore know which subjects, if any, are closest to the next band upwards. It is logical to appeal those subjects, rather than the one you feel you should have done better in.

The SEC issues the results of Leaving Certificate appeals in early October and final offers of places by the CAO based on these results will be made up to mid-October.

Remember

Remember that your grades fall in bands of 5%. If 18% on average succeed with an appeal then it is statistically probable that those who secure an upgrade are students who appeal and who are within 1% of the next grade.

Section 2

13 Post Leaving Certificate (PLC) Courses

Post Leaving Certificate (PLC) courses are offered at a local level throughout the country in colleges under the control of sixteen Education Training Boards (ETBs). The boards were established in 2013 and replaced the thirty-three Vocational Education Committees (VECs).

SOLAS, the new Further Education and Training Authority in Ireland, will coordinate and fund the activities of the ETBs from 2014 onwards. Replacing FÁS, SOLAS manages a wide range of further education and training opportunities, including apprenticeships and eCollege.

The ETBs' range of services will be available to you in your local region, after you complete your Leaving Certificate exams in August.

Benefits of PLC Courses

✓ One of the significant advantages of taking a PLC course as opposed to a CAO programme is the cost. All CAO courses carry a €3,000 registration charge, unless you qualify for a grant through SUSI. PLC courses on the other hand tend to cost €200–€600 at most.

✓ As the PLC colleges are located in every ETB area you can usually commute to them from home, saving you the cost of accommodation. This is often a prohibitive cost for those attending a CAO programme in a University or Institute of Technology.

✓ Means-tested maintenance grants are available to PLC students. Apply early to studentfinance.ie.

Finding the Right PLC Course

The old FÁS training structure is now being amalgamated with the Post Leaving Certificate colleges, within each of the sixteen Education and Training Boards. The opportunities on offer to you every September will be changing far more quickly than in past years. You need to become familiar with what is being proposed by your local ETB and how these courses will be offered. You can access this information online. For example the Donegal ETB (www.donegalvec. ie) now includes the former SOLAS centres which have become Training Centre Letterkenny and Training Centre Gaoth Dobhair.

Students who may be interested in training for a trade or skill will also have to find out what is on offer in their local area through their local ETB.

1. The website www.qualifax.ie has a PLC section under its course listings. You can explore hundreds of courses on offer by searching course types such as Hairdressing, Fire and Ambulance, Hotel and Catering, Tourism and Travel and so on.

2. You can search the entire country or confine your search to a single county.

3. The site looks at the course content and the employment opportunities as well as academic progression routes open to students who successfully complete the course.

4. If you identify a course that attracts your interest, you can follow-up this search by contacting the colleges on their own websites, where an online application form is always available.

Most PLC colleges currently offer 6th Year students numerous opportunities to visit the college during Open Days. They will also usually be more than happy to visit your school to meet with a group of students who may be interested in attending their courses. Just ask your guidance counsellor to organise a visit.

PLCs & Your Career Journey

- Each year, it is estimated, thousands of 6th Year students throughout Ireland who have applied to the CAO will not secure sufficient points in the Leaving Certificate to be offered a place on the course of their choice. As they may not want to accept the course they are offered, these students may end up considering a Level 5/6 course instead.

- If you do take up a PLC course you will be marked on eight modules, for which you may be awarded a pass, merit or distinction. As in the Leaving Certificate, it is the student who secures a high number of distinctions who stands the best chance of gaining an entry level position with an employer or a college CAO place if that is your goal.

- Many more students may get a satisfactory CAO offer but they may not be in a financial position to take up a place. This could be because of having to live away from home or not qualifying for a grant and being unable to pay the €3,000 registration charge. Depending on their circumstances these students could do a PLC course until they get their finances sorted out.

14 Employment

For students who are not interested in pursuing any form of further academic study, including PLC courses, apprenticeships and third level options, finding employment after the Leaving Certificate examination will be the first natural step on their career journey.

The job market is a competitive place so it's essential that you have a strong Curriculum Vitae (CV) and Letter of Application before you start contacting prospective employers or recruitment agencies.

Preparing Your CV

If a job opportunity arises you will have to be ready to present yourself in the best possible light:

- At a minimum you should always have a template of your CV ready to edit to ensure that it is formatted specifically with your prospective employer in mind.

- Never present a CV to any prospective employer without visiting the company's website, reading about it and working out what message it wants to represent to the public. Unless some references to the company's goals, philosophy and objectives are reflected in your CV it will probably go straight in the bin.

There are thousands of websites to assist you in drafting a CV, if you have not already learnt how to put one together. The most useful template you can use is the Europass as it will be familiar to potential employers throughout Europe. Its standard CV format will allow you to detail your qualifications and skills in a straightforward way. (See www.europass.ie.)

Top Tip!

Remember, less than 5% of CVs ever make it to the interview stage, and if your CV is not of the highest quality, without ANY spelling mistakes, you are wasting your time in submitting it.

Letter of Application

You also need to know how to write a simple letter to accompany your CV. Again, a well structured document, with clear, concise sentences and paragraphs, in which you state who you are and why you are interested in an entry level position in a particular company or organisation, will impress any prospective employer.

The fact that you have gone to the bother of visiting the website, and reflecting this in your application, will ensure that if the employer is considering recruiting young apprentices or other entry-level trainees, you have a good chance of being called to present yourself for interview.

Look at the tips below:

- Address your letter to a specific person whenever possible and make sure to spell names correctly.

- Be concise and stick to relevant facts. Say which job you are applying for and why your experience makes you a good fit for the position.

- Refer to the areas of your CV that match the job requirements (that is, your qualifications and relevant experience).

Top Tip!

Cover letters should be to the point. Keep the letter to one page if possible but definitely no longer than two pages.

Q. How can I make my application stand out?

A. Highlight your strengths. Prospective employers want to know why they should consider you for the position above anyone else. Show how your skills, talents and experience in jobs that you may have had during school holidays would be a valuable addition to the company.

Q. How should I end the letter?

A. Be proactive. Say that you look forward to hearing from the employer and that you are available for interview. Give your email and your home, work and mobile numbers, and make sure you are available. Keep your phone close at hand and check your emails regularly.

Useful Websites

The websites below have useful tips and sample cover letters that you can adapt for your own use.

✓ www.writeon.ie

✓ www.monster.ie

✓ www.careersportal.ie

✓ www.tcd.ie/Careers/students/jobsearch

✓ www.jobsearch.com

How to Succeed at an Interview

Thousands of Leaving Certificate students have to attend interviews each year during February and March. Some do so as part of a UCAS application, others as part of an application process for entry into a continental EU university programme. Many more are interviewed as part of the assessment process for a restricted application course within the CAO or because they have applied for a Post Leaving Certificate programme. Some scholarship programmes, be they academic, sports, or the arts, also involve an interview.

If you want to apply to a financial institution for a loan to help you fund your undergraduate studies you will also have to present yourself to make your case. Therefore it is vitally important that you know how to perform well at an interview.

1. Don't go on the tear the night before an interview. I once turned up to do an interview on TV alongside a young man who was a student on a scholarship programme with a major employer. He had got involved in some altercation the previous night that had left him with a black eye. The public relations official from his employer was less than impressed.

2. It may seem old fashioned, but any interviewer is impressed if the candidate has obviously gone to the bother of getting a haircut, putting on clean, neat clothing, polished their shoes and cleaned their teeth. For males a jacket, shirt and tie, and grey or black trousers is the norm. For females, a blouse with a skirt to the knee or a pair of trousers is perfectly acceptable. Remember, you are there to make an impression and discuss the details of your CV or letter of application. This is not a social occasion, so dress accordingly.

3. Arrive before your interview time to allow for unexpected delays. Nothing is worse than arriving flustered and hot and then having to sit in front of an interview panel for twenty minutes.

4. Everybody you meet once you enter the interview area may be part of the eventual decision on your application, so be conscious of everything you say or do once you arrive.

5. When you enter the room, shake hands politely with the interviewer and with each member of the interview board if there is more than one interviewer. Sit down when directed to do so, placing your two feet firmly on the ground in front of you.

6. When asked a question answer concisely, addressing your reply to the person who asked you the question, without holding them in a locked eyeball stare. As you respond, don't forget to move your head to include anyone else on the interview panel.

7. Never lie in an interview situation as your discomfort will always show. You will invariably get a follow-up question that will expose your lie

and destroy your chances of succeeding in your objective. An interview panel is far more impressed with young people who say that they don't understand the question or that they do not as yet have enough experience to answer informatively.

Useful Websites

The websites below offer advice on how to prepare for interviews and the types of questions asked.

- ✓ www.monster.co.uk
- ✓ www.ehow.com
- ✓ www.wikijob.co.uk
- ✓ www.writeon.ie

- ✓ www.youtube.com
- ✓ www.recruitireland.com/careercentre
- ✓ www.publicjobs.ie

8. If at the end of the interview process you are invited to ask a question you should have prepared at least one question as this shows again that you have thought about the interview. A question that shows a familiarity with the activities of the organisation conducting the interview impresses.

9. When you are informed that the interview is over and are being escorted from the room, be aware that you are still being observed. Many interviewees let their guard down at this stage thinking the process is over – a big mistake.

Getting Help

There are a number of new initiatives and supports available that can assist you as you start looking for your first job.

Skills to Work

www.skillstowork.ie

Skills to Work is a new Irish Government jobs website, aimed at making it easier for jobseekers and employers to know what Government skills initiatives are available to them.

The purpose of this website is to encourage businesses to employ people currently on the Live Register. If you are a registered unemployed jobseeker it will also help you to secure employment.

An online tool with a series of simple questions has been developed to direct jobseekers to information on what education, re-skilling or work experience options are available to them in areas of new and emerging employment opportunities.

Points to note

As a second level student none of these programmes are available to you immediately, as you are not currently a registered unemployed person. You can apply for them only if you have been registered with the Department of Social Protection as an unemployed person for a certain defined period of time. (See pages 80–84 for more information.)

1 Springboard

www.springboardcourses.ie

Springboard provides free, part-time and flexible higher education re-skilling courses at certificate, degree and masters level in areas where there are skills shortages, such as ICT and entrepreneurship. It is open to unemployed and previously employed people who are actively seeking employment.

More than 18,000 jobseekers have taken up a Springboard place (including the ICT Skills Conversion Courses) since 2011 and a further round of 6,100 free higher education places was made available to jobseekers in June 2014.

2 Momentum

www.momentumskills.ie

Co-financed by the EU, MOMENTUM funds the provision of free training projects to allow the long-term unemployed to gain skills and access work opportunities in identified growth sectors. The categories where projects are funded include construction, ICT, transport, distribution and logistics, tourism, financial services and manufacturing (technology).

Over 6,500 places were made available through Momentum in 2013 and a further round of this programme will be launched in 2014. Information on how to apply and the courses available can be found on the website.

3 JobBridge

www.jobbridge.ie

JobBridge assists individuals in breaking the cycle where they are unable to get a job because they don't have any work experience. JobBridge provides internship opportunities of either six or nine months.

The scheme is open to unemployed people at all education and skills levels who are in receipt of certain social welfare payments or are signing on for credits for at least three of the last six months (78 days).

Interns receive an allowance of €50 per week on top of their existing social welfare entitlement. This is payable for the period of their internship.

4 Skillnets

www.skillnets.ie/training

Skillnets supports the training needs of Irish businesses, employees and job-seekers through up to sixty training networks nationwide, across a range of sectors and regions. Skillnets actively supports and works with businesses in Ireland to address their current and future skills needs.

Up to 8,000 Skillnets' places are offered to jobseekers annually in a diverse range of education and training programmes and work placement in areas of employment potential.

5 JobsPlus

www.jobsplus.ie

JobsPlus is an employer incentive scheme that encourages and rewards employers who offer full-time jobs to the long-term unemployed. Monthly cash payments are made to qualifying employers to offset wage costs.

There are two levels of cash incentives:

✓ A payment of €10,000 over two years to an employer for each person recruited who has been unemployed for more than two years.

✓ A payment of €7,500 over two years for each person recruited who has been unemployed for more than 12 months but less than 24 months.

15 Apprenticeships

The benefits of developing a set of skills that will facilitate you in securing high quality employment for your working life are self-evident.

Earn and Learn

Students face a challenging job market. Kara McGann from Ibec has this advice for jobseekers: 'Education and experience are critically important when competing in today's competitive workplaces and many candidates may lack one or other of these key elements.

For some of you the first step on your career journey after school will be to college or university. For others, apprenticeships will be your first step towards achieving career success as they offer you a direct route into the employment market where you can earn a salary at the same time that you acquire qualifications.'

New Structures for Apprenticeships

If your parents/guardians are advising you about your transition from post-primary education to working life they may be using phrases such as getting a start in a trade, traditional apprenticeships in the construction industry, work your time and so on. All of this is now in the process of change.

FÁS has been dissolved and the new SOLAS authority is responsible for the statutory apprenticeship system in co-operation with the Department of Education and Skills, employers and unions. Following a review of apprenticeship training in Ireland published in December 2013 new types of apprenticeships, which will provide you with the skills to work in high technology sectors, are being developed. Employers in these sectors will be looking to identify young, flexible workers with generic transferable skills, such as literacy, numeracy, IT and people skills.

The Government plan is to co-opt employers in your locality so that they become involved in the design of new apprenticeship models, based on providing training within the new ETB college structures, as well as work placements with a local employer. When it is implemented the new system should provide you with far more effective ways of acquiring the skills you need to secure regular, high quality employment throughout your working life.

If such a career pathway is of interest to you, keep your eyes and ears open over the coming months for opportunities that may arise in your local area and consult the SOLAS website at www.solas.ie.

What Does an Apprenticeship Involve?

All apprenticeships lead to an award at Level 6 Advanced in the National Framework of Qualifications (NFQ):

- Currently this involves a seven stage on-and-off-the-job training programme over three years before you become a fully qualified tradesperson yourself.
- The employer meets the cost of on-the-job training for 170 of the 201 weeks of all apprenticeship programmes, and pays you a wage during that period.
- The State bears the cost of the forty weeks of off-the-job training and the cost of your wages for this period.

If the Government follows through on implementing the recommendations on the review of apprenticeship training you may find new models of apprenticeship being developed for technical roles in areas of growth in the economy such as ICT, medical devises, pharmaceuticals, biotechnology, food and drink, engineering, financial services, business and marketing.

Benefits of Becoming an Apprentice

What are the benefits of deciding to undertake an apprenticeship after my Leaving Certificate?

✓ Apprenticeships offer an opportunity for you to 'test drive' a career to see if it is a good fit, and you benefit from hands-on learning.

Top Tip!

'Apprenticeships offer real employment experience, on-and-off-the-job learning, preparation for a specific occupation, a nationally recognised qualification – all combined with being paid while you are studying.'
Kara McGann, Ibec

Apprenticeships are already offered in twenty-five areas at a Level 6 stage including engineering, motor, electrical, construction and print (see list on page 155). As part of the 2013 review the Government is working to extend this to a much broader range of occupations. The new model will incorporate qualifications from Levels 5–10, i.e. intermediate and advanced apprenticeships, which will deliver skills that reflect the needs of the Irish economy.

Apprentices develop a range of transferable skills which support job progression or further higher education.

✓ You will graduate with practical and technical skills that are relevant in a global market, along with a clear perspective on the nature of your profession.

✓ Apprentices develop professional, technical and communication skills in a business environment. You will have the opportunity to apply theoretical academic knowledge in a work environment while you are training.

✓ You will have the opportunity to develop many important 'employability' skills including teamwork, critical thinking, problem-solving and communication skills.

✓ After graduation apprentices have an advantage over a lot of potential competitors for jobs as they are well rounded individuals, with both qualifications and real work experience. They are also familiar with an employer's expectations which improves their job interview skills.

✓ For employers, apprenticeships offer a tried and tested way to recruit and develop skilled employees, giving them access to a broad, diverse talent pool and helping them develop competencies for the future.

- **Apprenticeships are not for students who don't have the points' to go to university.** These are challenging programmes that can provide a real alternative to university for those who want to go straight into work. If you get high points there is no requirement for you to only consider university – many companies are looking to recruit ambitious school-leavers who want to work while they learn.

- Choosing the apprenticeship route does not mean that you are turning your back on higher education. Apprenticeships will offer qualifications ranging from Level 5 to Level 9 depending on the industry, and the training cost will be covered.

Existing Apprenticeship Trades

Construction Sector	Brick & Stone Laying
	Carpentry & Joinery
	Floor & Wall Tiling
	Painting & Decorating
	Plastering
	Plumbing
	Wood Manufacturing & Finishing
Electrical Sector	Electrical
	Electrical Instrumentation
	Instrumentation
	Refrigeration & Air Conditioning
	Aircraft Mechanics
	Electronic Security Systems
Motor Sector	Agricultural Mechanics
	Construction Plant Fitting
	Heavy Vehicle Mechanics
	Motor Mechanics
	Vehicle Body Repairs
Engineering Sector	Mechanical, Automation and Maintenance Fitting (MAMF)
	Metal Fabrication
	Sheet Metalwork
	Tool Making
	Industrial Insulation
	Farriery
Printing Sector	Print Media

Apprenticeships in the Craft Industry

There is a wide range of career opportunities available in the craft industry for the artistic or creative young person. You could consider a future working with materials such as:

Metal – to become a jeweller, silversmith, goldsmith, blacksmith or farrier there are third level courses and apprenticeships of three to four years on offer.

Wood – to do woodturning, furniture design and furniture making or basket making, you could study as an apprentice for three to four years.

Glass – to train as a glassmaker or glass artist there are courses ranging from one year up to four years for specialist degree programmes.

Clay – to train as a ceramicist, potter, ceramic artist or designer there are third level courses of three to four years available.

Textiles – to become a textile artist/ designer or a fashion designer you could choose from a range of third level courses or apprenticeships of three to four years.

There are three primary providers of craft education outside of higher education institutions – **ETBs**, **City & Guilds** and the **Crafts Council of Ireland**. A full list of course providers across all craft disciplines is available on the Craft Council website (www.ccoi.ie).

16 Studying Abroad

For those of you who will achieve over 500 points in your Leaving Certificate results, securing your course choice close to home may not be a problem. But there are many professions and career pathways that are completely out of reach in Irish colleges for student who secures 300–500 points.

If you are willing to look at securing a place in another EU University or in a third level institution in the USA, Australia or New Zealand you should be able to find a solution to the points problem. Yet, only a tiny proportion of you will ever consider courses outside the commuting distance from your home, never mind in another EU country.

Just as many highly-motivated students in the USA research course choices throughout the entire country, you should be broadminded when considering what you want to do next year. Think outside the box a little.

Students today are being referred to as the first generation of 'global citizens', as low-cost travel and the internet make national borders increasingly irrelevant, in terms

Points to note

All reputable colleges throughout the world set minimum academic standards which students must meet before they are offered a place. In Ireland Matriculation is the term used to define the standard required to secure a place on most undergraduate degrees. It requires a learner to secure two higher level C3s, plus four ordinary level D3s at Leaving Certificate level.

Very few potential learners are aware that this is the required standard to secure an Irish college place because from the mid-1970s the supply of suitably qualified applicants holding matriculation standard and above, far exceeds the numbers of places on offer in most university courses. Since that date a further competition has taken place among the suitably qualified applicants – the points race – which shuts out a large portion of candidates from their desired course. Private education has grown to over 12 per cent of the third level sector in response to the demands of the disappointed students.

of sourcing jobs, lifestyle purchases, social networks, education and friendships. So, unsurprisingly, more and more Irish students are looking to source undergraduate (and postgraduate) opportunities beyond our borders. This is particularly relevant as our own system is coming under pressure, in terms of resources, quality and places.

Why Go to University in Continental Europe?

In recent years, Irish students are going to universities in a range of countries across Continental Europe. The most popular European destinations for Irish students are: the Netherlands, Denmark and Germany. Students have secured places in public European universities, particularly in programmes in Psychology, Politics, Business, Liberal Arts & Sciences and International Law.

The numbers of Irish students accessing these programmes has grown for the following reasons:

1 Programmes Are Taught in English

Until recently, most of the students travelling overseas for an education sourced university places in English-speaking countries, such as the UK or the USA. Continental Europe has not been considered because the vast majority of students would rather not do a degree in French or German or any other European language – but now that's all changed.

Reflecting the globalisation of the world's economies, and the fact that, increasingly, the international language of the business, engineering, IT and science sectors, and many other areas, is English, many Research Universities in Continental Europe, and Universities of Applied Sciences (their equivalent to our Institutes of Technology), are offering undergraduate degree programmes taught through English.

The acute shortage of young people throughout Continental Europe has also facilitated this development as colleges try to attract applicants from outside their domestic market. It's a simple matter of biology. Family size in most Continental EU countries is below replacement levels and has been for decades. Their third level institutions struggle to attract sufficient students to fill their courses. Conversely, the number of young people in Ireland is growing constantly so there is going to be increasing pressure on college places and higher entry points requirements in the years ahead.

There are currently about 900 programmes available, across Europe, in a full range of subjects (see listings on www.eunicas.ie) and this number is growing every year. Irish students are already attending these universities, studying courses such as Business Management, Natural Sciences, Medicine, Chemical Engineering, Psychology, Veterinary Science, Liberal Arts, Physiotherapy, International Law, Game Design, International Relations and many more.

Top Tip!

In 2012 the University of Groningen in the Netherlands switched teaching of all undergrad programmes in its Faculty of Maths & Natural Sciences from Dutch to English, reflecting the fact that in the twenty-first century the language of Science is English.

2 You Can Fast-track Your Employment Prospects

A good degree from a reputable university provides you with a skill set that meets the needs of employers. The quality of your education, together with your international experience, perspective and networks, will make your CV stand out, in the minds of both global companies and local companies seeking to internationalise their products, services and markets.

For those seeking to enter the professions here, qualifications obtained in Continental Europe, in areas such as Medicine, Physiotherapy, Nursing and Veterinary Science are recognised by the relevant professional bodies in Ireland and the UK.

3 You Can Access High Quality Education and Training

Many of the universities offering these programmes such as the University of Warsaw, or the Charles University in Prague, are highly-ranked universities. For example, Utrecht University in the Netherlands is ranked 1st in the Netherlands, 13th in Europe and 52nd in the world by the prestigious *Shanghai Academic Rankings of World Universities* 2013. Seven of the Dutch Universities are higher ranked than Trinity College Dublin. Also, most of the Universities and Universities of Applied Sciences are very well resourced and offer fabulous facilities to students.

Across the various disciplines the use of problem-based learning is very common as it encourages students to take some responsibility for their learning, rather than sitting passively in lecture halls.

4 Cost Is Not a Factor

Many people assume that studying abroad is expensive. This is not necessarily so in Continental Europe where all EU citizens must be treated equally when it comes to third level costs. Unlike the €3,000 registration costs in Ireland, the following applies to fees in universities across Europe:

- Tuition is currently free in Denmark, Norway, Finland, Sweden and Malta though this is subject to change.
- In Iceland there are no tuition fees for EU students but there is an annual registration fee of approx. €490.
- Fees between €600–3,000 plus apply in Italy, where tuition fees are fixed with reference to family income. The average Irish student pays €900 per annum, including if they are studying Medicine.
- Fees of €1,906 upwards are charged for all programmes in the Netherlands, with a supplement of €1,000 for Liberal Arts & Sciences programme. All EU citizens can claim a low-interest Tuition Fee Loan from the Dutch government to repay the full fee cost with a fifteen-year repayment period after graduation.
- In Germany and Austria some courses have free fees while others charge up to €1,500.
- Tuition fee loans are also available in Bulgaria, covering fees for some Medical and Veterinary programmes, where yearly fees are approx. €5,500 to €8,000.

In some countries, e.g. Denmark and the Netherlands, you can access subsistence grants, but you will usually need a part-time job to qualify for these. Of course if you qualify for an Irish Maintenance Grant, you can take it with you to public universities in the EU.

- Living costs? Apart from the traditionally expensive cities such as Copenhagen or Paris, costs are usually lower than living in Dublin, and equivalent to, though often lower than, living in Cork.

5 Entry Requirements Are Very Reasonable

Most EU countries work on the basis that you have a right to a third level education, without selecting you through points or grades. For example, Dutch universities are forbidden, by statute, from basing their selection procedures on grades.

Across Europe the grade requirements will invariably be much lower than here, though in the most popular programmes, e.g. Medicine, Psychology or Physiotherapy, there is a selection procedure. This might include a test or an interview or you might have to submit a Letter of Motivation or a Letter of Recommendation from your school or a combination of one or more of these options.

6 **Have an Adventure!**

You should have fun at university, whether you go to one here, on the Continent or further afield. For many students the sense of adventure deepens when you find yourself in a cobbled square, in a medieval Italian city, looking up at a Palazzo, thinking of what you are going to do that night, after you have finished your Global Medicine assignment.

Give it a go!

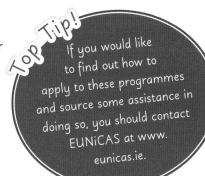

Top Tip!
If you would like to find out how to apply to these programmes and source some assistance in doing so, you should contact EUNiCAS at www.eunicas.ie.

Entry Requirements

Unlike Ireland, most continental European systems are focused on providing a university-level education to as wide a number of students as possible. Achieving good grades in your Leaving Certificate is not necessarily a requirement to secure a place in an EU degree programme as many colleges have their own entry criteria.

Points to note

Students are expected to take the right to education seriously when they start their study programme, so if you do not commit fully to your studies in first year you are likely to be coming home for good at the end of the summer term.

✓ Six Italian medical schools offer Medicine programmes taught through English and are not interested in Leaving Certificate grades as they select exclusively based on their own entrance test – IMAT.

✓ Dutch universities, excluding Liberal Arts & Sciences colleges, are forbidden by law to select based on grades/points. Many programmes have no limits on places and will admit you if you hold a National University of Ireland matriculation.

✓ Some European courses have a limit on places, e.g. Physiotherapy and Psychology, which select students through a combination of interviews and letters of motivation plus in some cases, preferred grades such as 400-450 CAO points required for Physiotherapy. Psychology degree programmes often require you to sit an aptitude test.

✓ Higher level maths is required for many, but not all, programmes in research universities, with ordinary level accepted for most other programmes where maths is not a taught subject.

✓ Most high quality Spanish universities are an exception and select students based on their grades which often have to be quite high.

The Next Step

If you have established that you have the minimum requirements for the course of your choice and you are going to apply to a university in Continental Europe, you need to consider the following:

1 Research your university carefully. Some independent advisors, e.g. www. learnabroad.ie, can be very helpful; avoid so-called 'advisors' who charge you for their assistance.

2 Visit the university yourself before you commit to the course. Airfares to Central Europe are very reasonable.

3 Get in touch with Irish students who are already studying there and ask for their feedback.

4 Find out about drop-out rates. For example, there have been suggestions that these are high in Hungary.

5 Test the levels of spoken English of teaching staff by contacting them.

6 Establish the levels of student support on the administration side. Sometimes the levels of communication between the university and students can be poor.

7 It is also worth checking the quality of on-campus accommodation.

Top Tip!
For more information on Hungary see www.studyhungary.ie and on everything else see www. learnabroad.ie.

In summary, most of the English-language university programmes provide genuine opportunities for Irish students to achieve third level qualifications that would not otherwise be available to them, particularly if they want to qualify as doctors or vets.

Applying for a Place

Applying for a place in an EU university can be a time consuming activity:

- Only four EU countries – the Netherlands, Denmark, Sweden and Finland – have some level of centralised application procedure, akin to our CAO system.

- There are centralised qualification validation requirements in Germany and Spain.

- Many Dutch universities have different application deadlines, with faculties at the same university also imposing diverse deadlines. For example, the earliest cut-off date is 1 February for Liberal Arts & Science programmes with selection procedures in March/April; while other courses remain open until after the Leaving Certificate results are published in August.

- All Finnish and many Swedish universities require the submission of examination results by July at the latest. This means that most Irish and UK students interested in courses in those two countries will need to take a gap year.

- In Denmark the application deadline is in mid-March.
- In a number of EU countries applicants apply directly to the university or to the qualification validation body or to the authority organising the entrance test.

Given this disparate application process, many students and their families find the EUNiCAS application support service useful and reassuring. Eunicas.ie contains details on every course offered through English and gives general advice on programme choice, application guidelines and forms, past exam papers where relevant, application document review, and assistance in organising university visits. (See pages 54–56 for more information.)

Studying Medicine in Central Europe

Over recent years, students have increasingly become aware of opportunities in Central Europe – Hungary, Poland, Czech Republic and Slovakia – to study Medicine on degree programmes taught through English.

The first English-language programmes were launched in the early 1990s and the first courses in Semmelweis University, Budapest and Charles University, Prague, were targeted at US students. They are now popular with English-speaking students from across Europe and further afield.

It has been suggested that Charles and Semmelweis universities might be resting on their laurels and they are certainly the most expensive options. This has provided the incentive for a growing number of other universities to develop their own programmes including:

- Czech Republic – Masaryk
- Hungary – Pecs, Debrecen and Zseged
- Poland – Jagiellonian in Krakow and the Medical Faculties in Warsaw, Lodz and Poznan
- Slovakia – PJSU Kosice and Commenius

Annual fees at these universities are from €8,500 upwards. Other than in Semmelweis and Charles, the largest numbers of Irish students seem to be found in PJSU Kosice and the University of Debrecen.

Grace, a Second-year Medicine Student in PJSU Kosice in Slovakia, enthuses:

> I'm a med student. I still can't believe it! It's the end of my first year already! It's probably been the best year of my life!! The different culture, country, people .... I have friends from every corner of the planet nearly and it's absolutely amazing! And of course I'm studying hard as well. But it gets harder towards the summer finals! I love it here .... I've settled in so well. I love my studies and there's great craic to be had as well ..... All our international friends got together to celebrate St Patrick's Day with us – it was great!

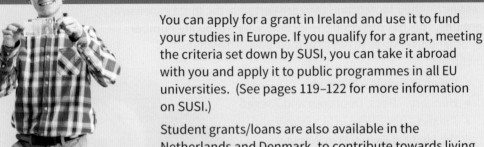

The MD degrees in all of the above universities are recognised by the Medical Council. But remember that you still have to secure an intern year back in Ireland or the UK, after you graduate in Central Europe.

> It is almost fifteen years now since the first wave of Irish students began to access fee-paying programmes in Veterinary and Medicine in Central European Universities in Hungary, Poland and the Czech Republic. The community of Irish students in Budapest is now so large that they have established their own GAA club.

Grants

You can apply for a grant in Ireland and use it to fund your studies in Europe. If you qualify for a grant, meeting the criteria set down by SUSI, you can take it abroad with you and apply it to public programmes in all EU universities. (See pages 119–122 for more information on SUSI.)

Student grants/loans are also available in the Netherlands and Denmark, to contribute towards living expenses, subject to students also working part-time.

STUDYING IN THE USA

Each year over 1,000 Irish students go to college in the USA, where there are over 4,000 third level colleges.

Most colleges have application deadlines around the middle of 6th Year, so students should begin preparing to apply as early as possible – see the timetable below!

6th Year Timeframe	Enrolment Countdown	Action Plan
Autumn of 6th Year – before mid-term break	10–12 Months	• Learn about the US higher education and application process. Visit www.educationusa.info and make sure that studying in the US is right for you. • Begin researching universities – there are over 4,000 to choose from. • Finalise your selection of four to six universities. • SAT Test: If you have not already taken your SAT you should apply to do so and sit it by December at the latest. Irish students should register through www.Collegeboard.com at least six weeks in advance. • Request a transcript from your school and two or three reference letters. • Draft your application essays. • Begin admissions and funding applications.
Autumn of 6th Year – after mid-term break	8–10 Months	• Submit admisions applications for 4–6 US colleges by the deadline. • Submit funding applications for financial aid and scholarships as early as possible. You need to list your SAT results on your submission. Deadlines vary depending on the institution and some operate on a rolling basis so you may be able to apply later in the year.
Spring of 6th Year	4–7 Months	• Receive admissions decisions – usually provisional and based on your final Leaving Certificate results.

Summer after Leaving Certificate Exams	1–3 Months	• Notify universities . • Apply for your visa. • Read the Pre-Departure Section of Fulbright website.
August/ September		• Begin study in the US!

Applying to a US College

The application process will involve:

✓ Identifying prospective colleges.

✓ Taking the Scholastic Aptitude Test (SAT) exams.

✓ Ensuring involvement in extracurricular activities, such as sports or volunteering.

✓ Completing a comprehensive application within the deadline.

Colleges in America utilise a holistic process when they review student applications, which means that they look at more than just grades. This system will suit students who may have struggled previously, but have since improved.

Irish students considering applying to the USA should consider the following:

Points to note

The American college applications system may initially seem daunting. Supported by the US Department of State, Education USA is the only official advisory service in Ireland and source of information on educational opportunities in the US. It is based in the Fulbright Commission. If you want more information about Education USA email educationusa@fulbright.ie.Information on applying to colleges in the US can also be found on www.fulbright.ie.

1 Which are the best colleges?

There is no official ranking system for colleges and universities in the US. To check the accreditation status of a school see www.chea.org or search world university rankings at www.timeshighereducation.co.uk and www.shanghairanking.com.

2 What is different about US colleges?

- There are two types of colleges to choose from:
  - Four-year public/private colleges – undergraduate degrees and postgraduate degrees.
  - Two-year community/junior colleges – associate degrees. Many offer students the opportunity to transfer onto an affiliated four-year college for the final two years so students can get a Bachelors Degree. This is known as the 2+2 format.

Top Tip!

When applying to US colleges you will be asked to provide official school transcripts from 5th Year and even from your Junior Certificate.

- Unlike the CAO process, students do not have to decide what they want to study right away. Instead, students study a broad range of subjects early on, known as the Liberal Arts and then focus on their Major in later years.
- You should also consider the following potential differences:

  - Is it a big city campus or university town campus?
  - What type of climate is it?
  - What's the student to faculty ratio?
  - Are there opportunities to do undergraduate research?

Luckily there are plenty of useful search engines that can help students narrow the search for US colleges. You should contact the EducationUSA office for more advice and to link into search engines. Visit their website www.fulbright.ie or call them on 01-6607670. Another excellent resource is www.educationUSA.info.

3 What is the SAT?

To get into US colleges you need to take a standardised test. There are two types: the SAT (Scholastic Aptitude Testing) and the ACT (American College Testing) but there is currently no ACT testing centre in Ireland.

The SAT is an aptitude test that measures critical thinking skills; the total testing time is 3 hours and 45 minutes. As this system may be changing, check www.collegeboard.com for updates.

- When you find a college you are interested in attending, check the previous year's average SAT scores on its website. This will give you an idea of the test score you will need to achieve in order to gain entry.

- Many competitive universities will also require two or three SAT subject tests. They are one-hour, multiple-choice tests, offered in sixteen subjects: Literature, US and World History, Mathematics Level 1 & 2 and Biology, Chemistry, Physics, Chinese, French, German, Spanish, Modern Hebrew, Italian, Latin, Japanese, and Korean.
- Students can sit the SAT more than once at a cost of approx. $80 for each test. There are two testing centres in Ireland, St. Conleth's, Dublin and St. Andrews College, Dublin. You can choose your testing centre when you register through www.collegeboard.com.

4 What are the typical application requirements?

Generally you must apply to each US college individually. The list below outlines what is generally required:

1   A completed application form – found on the college website or through Common Application Form (a system which 456 US colleges are signed up to. For more information see www.commonapp.org).

2   Application fee – varies but usually between $50–100 per college.

3   Admission exam scores – SAT/ACT.

4   Two or three letters of reference – academic ones from someone in your secondary school and an extra-curricular one from e.g. your GAA coach or scout leader.

5   Transcripts from your secondary school.

6   Interview (on occasion) – this is often done on the phone and is required in some of the more competitive four-year colleges.

7   Some US colleges require a full medical prior to enrolment.

5 Do your Leaving Certificate results matter?

Yes! Although the timeline is different in the US and colleges will already have your SAT scores and applications, students will still be required to submit their Leaving Certificate results. Many offers are provisional and colleges will want to ensure you achieve the projected results you detailed on your application, so getting those grades should remain a top priority.

6 What are the potential costs?

Tuition fees can vary significantly as each university sets its own. This information should be readily available on the university's financial aid or undergraduate admissions webpage.

As an international student, you will be considered an out-of-state student. The average tuition fees depend on the type of institution:

- For out-of-state students, at public four-year institutions the average rates are about $20,000 per year.
- For out-of-state students, at private four-year institutions the average rates are $30,000–$50,000 per year.
- For two-year colleges, you can expect fees to come to approximately $15,000–$18,000 per year.

US immigration regulations currently allow international students to work up to 20 hours per week on campus during their first year of study. On-campus jobs may include working at the cafeteria, bookstore, library, health club, or admin office.

You may apply for permission to work off campus for up to 20 hours a week after your first year. However, there is no guarantee that this request will be granted.

In your second year you can apply for employment as a resident assistant (RA) in an on-campus dormitory. An RA is the first point of contact for students who need assistance or have questions about campus life. They receive free accommodation and sometimes a small salary and/or meal plan.

Top Tip!

There is over $143 billion in financial aid available for study in the US, and approximately one in three international students reported a scholarship as their primary source of funding.

Studying in Australia and New Zealand

New Zealand and Australian universities offer thousands of courses in a vast range of subjects at undergraduate, postgraduate and doctoral level. What are some of the factors pulling students Down Under to study in universities in Australia and New Zealand?

1 Which are the best universities?

Australian and New Zealand universities are internationally prestigious and research-led. In the 2014 Academic Ranking of World Universities (ARWU) released by Shanghai Jiao Tong University, the University of Melbourne was ranked 44th and the Australian National University and University of Queensland are also ranked in the top 100 universities worldwide, while the University of Auckland is ranked in the top 200. To put this in an Irish perspective, in the same list TCD is the highest ranked Irish university at 170, while UCD is ranked at 254 and UCC is number 454.

The qualifications awarded by universities in Australia and New Zealand are recognised and respected by employers and other universities worldwide and at an undergraduate level are the direct equivalent of a European Bachelors degree.

❷ What is different about universities in Australia and New Zealand?

Many students base their choice of university destination on where they would like to live for a few years. After all, going to university isn't just about studying. As an international student you will have the freedom to live in New Zealand or Australia for the duration of your course. This will give you the opportunity to travel around and to immerse yourself in the culture.

Universities in Australia and New Zealand are very focused on the student experience, and offer a huge range of opportunities for you to maximise your time as a student. You can take part in an academic exchange and study almost anywhere in the world for a term or a year. Undertaking an internship and joining a voluntary project are also options.

There are also currently opportunities in both countries to stay on after finishing your degree and work. See www.studyoptions.com for more information on post-study work visa options.

❸ What's different about the courses?

General degrees – for example the Bachelor of Arts and Bachelor of Science – are typically much broader and more flexible in structure in Australia and New Zealand than is usually the case in Ireland. You have a much wider choice in terms of the subjects you study, and you can often create a programme that's uniquely tailored to your interests and career goals.

In certain subjects Australian and New Zealand universities are recognised as world leaders, including sport science, physiotherapy, geology, physical geography, social work, environmental science and marine studies. If you are working towards a career in one of these areas, studying in Australia or New Zealand could be the best possible start.

Both countries also offer students and researchers unparalleled access to the natural world and amazing opportunities for fieldwork. Marine scientists in Australia, for example, can use the Great Barrier Reef as a laboratory, or work in the waters of Tasmania, which are classed as the cleanest in the world, bar those of Antarctica.

❹ What are the likely costs?

The costs involved depend on the institution and can vary considerably between universities. As an international student, your tuition fees are payable before you study. The figures below are a guideline to the likely costs involved per year in Australia and New Zealand:

Australia		
	Undergraduate	Postgraduate
Arts	AU$18,000–AU$28,000	AU$18,000–AU$26,000
Commerce	AU$18,000–AU$31,000	AU$20,000–AU$33,000
Science	AU$19,000–AU$36,000	AU$20,000–AU$34,000

New Zealand		
	Undergraduate	Postgraduate
Arts	NZ$20,000–NZ$25,000	NZ$22,000–NZ$27,000
Commerce	NZ$21,000–NZ$26,000	NZ$23,000–NZ$30,000
Science	NZ$23,000–NZ$26,000	NZ$26,000–NZ$32,000

The fees listed above do not apply to high value courses such as Medicine and Veterinary. To get exact fees for any course visit the institution's website.

Make sure you research possible accommodation and living costs as well.

5 Are there good graduate job prospects?

Studying overseas will make your CV stand out to an employer. Many employers believe that moving abroad to study indicates that an applicant has initiative and independence. You will also have developed a valuable international perspective and network of contacts in Australia and New Zealand that could be a very valuable resource for Irish companies who want to expand their operations.

Top Tip!

Australian and New Zealand universities do offer international student scholarships. Almost all scholarships are awarded purely on academic merit; they are not given on the basis of financial need. You need to apply as early are possible. See www.studyoptions.com for more information.

1 Visit the website www.studyoptions.com. Study Options is the Irish and UK representative for many Australian and New Zealand universities and is responsible for helping Irish students make their course choices and applications. It is a free advice and application support service for students and schools.

2 Get a list of the courses available in your chosen subject from Study Options. You can contact this source at mail@ studyoptions.com

Make sure you specify:

- What area you want to focus on.
- If you've got any particular requests, e.g. if you want to be in a specific city.

The list will include weblinks to each course's content and structure, as well as details of tuition fees, entry requirements, application deadlines and other key information. Closing dates may vary according to the course for which you are applying.

3 Go through the list of courses carefully – check the weblinks, particularly the course breakdowns, and look around each university's website. Study Options also has prospectuses for all the universities, which you can get for free.

Research each university carefully, looking at e.g. student to faculty ratio, transport links, student accommodation. If possible get in touch with any Irish or other international students who are already studying there and ask them for feedback.

4 Once you've decided which universities you want to apply to, all the application forms and guides to completing them are available for download from the Study Options website. You can contact a student advisor for help if you need it.

Irish students apply to Australian and New Zealand universities using their Leaving Certificate results and are usually not required to take additional tests.

5 Send the completed applications to Study Options in London. This support service will check it to make sure everything is correct and complete, and sight and certify documents on behalf of the universities. Applications are then sent to the universities for assessment electronically.

Points to note

If you are successful and receive a Confirmation of Enrolment from your chosen university don't forget that anyone enrolling as an international student on a course lasting four months or more in Australia will need a student visa. If you are applying online you can only apply for your visa a maximum of 124 days before your course starts and can arrive in Australia up to 90 days before the starting date.

On a student visa you will be able to work up to 40 hours per fortnight during term and full-time in the holidays.

17 Scholarships

Scholarships come in two forms, those that provide you with a range of supports once you have been offered and have accepted a place in a specific college, and those that involve the college adding additional points to your initial CAO score based on your Leaving Certificate performance.

Why Do Colleges Offer Scholarships?

1 University Rankings

Third level colleges use scholarships to help them achieve the highest possible international academic ranking. The Shanghai Jiao Tong Academic Ranking of World Universities (ARWU) is published each year and details the top 500 universities worldwide. The Times Higher Education World University Rankings lists the top 400 universities.

Universities work tirelessly to attract the highest quality of undergraduate applicants to help improve their position on these rankings. Their scholarship programmes are an integral part of that process. Scholarships are in essence part of the marketing programme of each college.

✓ Academic scholarships are offered to attract the brightest and the best to a particular university.

✓ Sports scholarships are offered by third level institutions who want to try to attract elite sportspersons, across a wide range of sporting codes.

✓ Some colleges also offer scholarships in the performing arts for similar reasons.

Top Tip! Harvard University in the US is currently ranked number 1 in the Academic Ranking of World Universities.

2 Future Funding

Ireland's third level colleges, along with all such institutions worldwide, are huge business enterprises. They depend for their very survival on the public perception of them both within Ireland and internationally. Their alumni are scattered throughout the world and these former students are the life blood that sustain the colleges financially.

Many universities take the view that a student who achieves 625 points in their Leaving Certificate will have a higher probability of being in a financial position to contribute funding later in life than a 300 points student. Academic scholarships can be offered with this in mind.

3 International Students

Wealthy parents of prospective non-EU students in countries such as India and China, who have populations of over a billion each, closely monitor the ranking scores of universities worldwide before deciding which university to send their son or daughter to.

International students pay substantially large fees. For example, in Trinity College Dublin the non-EU tuition fee for a BA in Business Studies is €16,430, and in the University of Limerick the average non-EU fees for undergraduate courses in Science & Technology range from €10,000–€21,600. These fees help to meet the running costs associated with teaching domestic students, who pay relatively modest fees or charges. Attracting more academic students with scholarships means the university can achieve higher international rankings because such students tend to achieve First Class honours degrees.

4 Scholarships for Overseas Students

If you are looking at scholarship programmes overseas, in the US, Australia, New Zealand, Canada and so on, Internationalisation comes into play.

All universities worldwide want to attract a proportion of students from abroad because this meets one of the

criteria on which they are judged in published rankings. So, for instance, a good to average student in Ireland becomes a very attractive proposition to a mid-range university in the US and therefore worthy of an offer of a scholarship. The flip side of that is of course being far away from home, without the emotional support of many fellow Irish students. This also works in reverse as Irish universities can offer scholarships to international students for the same reason.

Irish Scholarships

Entrance Scholarships

Some universities and institutes of technology offer entrance scholarships based on your points score. If it is over a certain level, e.g. 500 points, you will receive a cash payment.

This may be confined to particular faculties or courses or it may be across all disciplines. For example:

- NUI Maynooth award entrance scholarships of €1,000 to each first-year student who achieves a minimum of 500 points.
- The UCD Entrance Exhibition is awarded to first year students who attain at least 540 points in the Leaving Certificate.
- IT Tralee offers a number of annual scholarship programmes including the Lee Strand Men's Gaelic Football Scholarships, Munster Council Bursary and the Muckross House Bursary (for students of BA (Hons.) in Folk Theatre).

- University of Limerick scholarships include: Paddy Dooley Rowing Club Scholarships – successful candidates are awarded €2,500 per annum, the Bank of Ireland Millennium Scholars Trust, the Intel Shannon Women in Technology Scholarship and the AIB Best Student Award in a range of subjects.

Elite Scholarship Programmes

If you are at a National or Inter-County level in a sporting discipline or in the performing arts you may wish to consider applying for an elite scholarship programme at any or all of the colleges that you intend listing on your CAO application.

Some universities now allow the successful student to secure a place on their nominated course on reduced points requirements. Colleges justify this policy on the basis of the time commitment required by applicants to achieve an international level of performance and acknowledge that this is bound to reduce the individual's capacity to achieve high grades in their Leaving Certificate and secure their maximum points potential.

- Within the Dublin region, University College Dublin, Dublin City University, and NUI Maynooth are matching each other in offering additional CAO points, up to a maximum of sixty, in a bid to secure the 'elite' in their respective disciplines. Trinity College Dublin does not offer any points concessions, but does support students who secure their places through the normal CAO points structure once they become students of the college.
- NUI Galway, which would compete with NUI Maynooth to attract students from the Midlands and North West, is currently offering up to forty additional CAO points to those it deems 'elite' in their field.
- The University of Limerick and University College Cork, as stand-alone universities in their respective regions, currently see no need to offer additional CAO points to aspiring sports or performing arts high-fliers.

The competition between colleges to attract the brightest and the best in all fields is an ongoing battle between all the third level institutions in the CAO system. The concessions currently offered may change and the scenario outlined above may be very different in a year's time, so always check with each college to find out what concessions it may be prepared to offer you in the year you apply.

Sports Scholarships in Irish Universities

The majority of third level institutes in Ireland offer a range of sports scholarship programmes which usually involve:

- Access at reduced cost to campus accommodation.
- Full access to all sports support and coaching services.
- Physiotherapy.
- Nutritional advice.
- Sports psychology.
- Medical support.
- Special arrangements regarding lectures and exams missed as a result of involvement in your sporting activities.

A selection of the sports' scholarships offered by Irish third level institutions are listed below. For more information consult each college's website.

University College Dublin (UCD)

UCD Sports Scholarship

This programme gives talented young people the opportunity of developing their sporting career by offering the highest standards in coaching, training, nutrition, and strength and conditioning advice, while they are completing their chosen course of study.

Benefits of the sports scholarship programme may include: access to the UCD High Performance Centre, free pool membership, access to on-campus accommodation, tuition fees, books, equipment, sport medicine and testing facilities, reduced physiotherapy costs, travel to national and international competitions and academic support.

The value and benefits of each sport scholarship is assessed on an individual basis. The assessments are conducted by UCD Sport and the relevant UCD club.

UCD's Elite Athlete Academy (EAA) & Ad Astra Academy

These academies provide a sixty point top-up for Leaving Certificate students identified for scholarships. The UCD Ad Astra academy also includes performing arts and academic scholars. There is a bursary of around €5,000 for elite athletes.

Candidates get an allowance towards the registration fee, part of the cost of accommodation is looked after and access to all the facilities on campus. They also get academic mentoring if they need any grinds, and if they are away with international teams/performances there is timetable flexibility.

NUI Maynooth

NUI Maynooth award a number of sports scholarships annually. High performance programmes are offered in GAA, golf, soccer, rugby and snooker. Consideration is also given to Irish Sports Council carded athletes.

The supports include expert coaching, fitness testing, physical conditioning/athletic therapy, sports psychology, performance analysis as well as regular

nutrition and lifestyle management seminars. Students receive financial support and priority access to on-campus accommodation. If necessary, they may receive additional academic support and are required to take all academic assessments as normal.

Eligible applicants must participate in an assessment and interview process. If they are successful they receive a concession of up to sixty points, from the CAO points required.

Students must meet the normal matriculation and special programme requirements and have attained at least 300 points (this concession is not available for NUI Maynooth's primary education degree).

Dublin City University (DCU)

DCU Sport Scholarship Programme

This programme is athlete led and grades its support on the athlete's achievement, potential and need. Athletes are allocated a sport scholarship at one of five levels, and up to a maximum of €3,000 in support services. These may include: membership to the university sports complex and high performance gym, 25m recovery pool, ice baths, indoor sprint track, flexibility studio, subsidised campus accommodation, financial support for academic fees, equipment, books, goal setting and performance planning, personal tuition where necessary, access to national and international elite competition, sports injury management, sports psychology and nutrition, biomechanical analysis.

DCU has also put in place a special academic entry scheme for elite sportspersons for all its undergraduate degree courses. A number of academic places will be reserved for outstanding candidates who have achieved a very high level of sporting performance and who are committed to continuing to develop their sporting and academic careers. Applications are not assessed solely on the basis of academic performance, but sporting achievements are also taken into consideration.

Eligible applicants, successful in the portfolio assessment and interview, may receive a small derogation of points, dependent on the programme, subject to a maximum of 60 points.

Students are required to meet the general and programme-specific entry requirements (this entry route is subject to review).

NUI Galway

Performance Points Scholarship

NUI Galway offers a sports scholarship programme that rewards athletes who are performing at the highest levels of their sport while also achieving academically. A limited number of scholarships will be offered for athletes who apply for courses that require more than 350 CAO points. Forty performance points will be on offer for successful candidates.

The benefits includes: a subsistence grant, coaching support, medical and physiotherapy support, performance nutrition, strength and conditioning and mentoring.

Elite Athlete Scholarship

This programme has been developed to assist young athletes to develop their sporting ability hand-in-hand with their academic progress by putting in place the necessary supports.

University College Cork (UCC)

University College Cork provides elite sportspersons with the opportunity to apply for a variety of sports scholarships whilst pursuing their academic and sporting careers.

Quercus Talented Students' Programme

Quercus, the Latin for oak, represents the nurturing philosophy that underpins the growth and development aspect of the programme, which offers gifted people scholarships worth up to €10,000 a year.

The programme will facilitate five elite athletes, along with a number of scholarships across the four other categories. Supports such as accommodation, fee payment, academic mentoring, book vouchers, support in nutrition, exercise physiology, coaching, physiotherapy, video analysis and so on will form part of this scholarship.

The scholarship will be developed around the individual's needs. Students interested in applying for the scholarships should visit www.ucc.ie/quercus.

Top Tip! Quercus Talented Students Programme: prospective and current UCC students can apply for scholarships in the following areas – academia active citizenship, creative and performing arts, innovation and entrepreneurship and sport.

UCC Sports Scholarships

UCC also annually awards sports scholarships ranging across a variety of sports. In 2013/14 twenty different sports clubs were represented on the scheme.

All successful applicants must represent UCC in their chosen sport. Further details are available on the website.

In addition to the UCC sports scholarships other targeted scholarships include:

- Cadburys U21 Gaelic Football – applications normally become available at the start of term. This scholarship is valued at €750 and is awarded to a student who plays inter-county at U21 level at a minimum.

- Jonathan Herlihy Memorial Scholarship – applications need to be sent directly to the Herlihy Foundation in Glanmire, Cork. These scholarships are available to applicants living in the Glanmire and surrounding areas. Up to four scholarships are awarded annually with a value of €1,000 each. This scheme is advertised locally.

- Roy Keane Soccer Scholarship and MJ Dowling Hurling Scholarship – further information available on www.ucc.ie/sport.

- Jason Foley Memorial Scholarship – part of the UCC application process, this scholarship is awarded to a basketball player and/or a student from the Carrigtwohill, Cork and surrounding district. It is valued at a minimum of €750 per annum.

- PSE Energy Kinsale Ltd Scholarship – awarded to a rugby player and valued at €1,000 per annum. It is awarded as part of the UCC Sports Scholarship Scheme.

- Three Kukri Scholarships – valued at €1,000 each per annum. No special application process. They are awarded as part of the UCC Sports Scholarship Scheme.

- Bank of Ireland Scholarships awarded to three first year students who have already excelled or have the potential in their chosen sport. Valued at €1,000 each, they are awarded as part of the UCC Sports Scholarship Scheme.

- Munster Council GAA – the Munster Council of the GAA also allocates bursaries to GAA students living in the Munster region. These bursaries are open to players and administrators and are valued at €750. Approximately twenty bursaries are allocated annually and this is determined by the Munster Council GAA and UCC.

University of Limerick (UL)

The University of Limerick does not currently offer any points concession to candidates awarded sports scholarships.

Michael Hillery and Jacinta O'Brien Athletics Scholarship

This scholarship is equivalent in value to €7,000. The benefits include: waiver of accommodation fees for campus-based accommodation, full membership of UL Arena and access to facilities, expert coaching, physiotherapy services, sports science support and nutritional advice, provision of a training expense grant valued at €500 per year. On qualification to the World University Games, UL may provide additional financial support to allow the athlete to travel and compete.

To be eligible for the scholarship candidates must meet at least one of the following criteria:

✓ Represent Ireland in Athletics at Senior Level during the year prior to application.

✓ Compete at World U20 or U23, European U20 or U23 championships during the year prior to application.

✓ Have won a medal in your event at Athletic Association of Ireland (AAI) National Senior Championships.

✓ Won the AAI National U20 or U23 championships.

Munster GAA Bursaries

The Munster Council of the GAA awards thirteen new bursaries each year to students from the province of Munster only, registered for Bachelor's Degree programmes at the University of Limerick.

New bursaries are initially awarded to first-year, full-time undergraduate students but students may re-apply for these bursaries in subsequent years of their degree programme. The value of each bursary is €1,000 per year.

Cadbury U21 Football Scholarships

To the value of €2,000 per university, these scholarships are presented to two full time UL students in recognition of their commitment to the sport, their high achievements to date and their potential.

Students applying for this programme must be on their U21 Football panels for the coming season.

UL/Bohemians Rugby Academy Bursaries

Each year a number of rugby bursaries are awarded to incoming full-time undergraduate students who satisfy the normal entry requirements.

The value of the bursaries ranges from €500 to €2,300, depending on rugby performance and experience.

Paddy Dooley Rowing Scholarship

The awarding of the rowing scholarship, which encompasses all undergraduate academic disciplines, will be based on rowing promise and Leaving Certificate results or academic performance.

The scholarship is for €2,500, is awarded annually and is open to full-time students from any year of undergraduate study at UL.

Limerick FC Talented Footballer Scheme (LTFS)

This is awarded to amateur association football players to support their sporting and educational development. LTFS works at three award levels:

1. First Team (up to €2,000)
2. A Championship and Ladies (up to €1,000)
3. U20 level (ladies' and men's (up to €500).

Support is also provided by way of access to training facilities (First Team only), physiotherapy and sport science support and a mentoring scheme.

Award levels are determined by specific performance standards and awards are made once a year. To apply go to www.limerickfc.ie.

Trinity College Dublin (TCD)

TCD offers a limited number of sporting scholarships to full-time students. Applicants should have outstanding ability in a particular sport and be willing to represent Trinity in their sport.

The scholarships provide the following benefits: monetary grant, nutritional workshops, physiological assessment/fitness testing and follow-up training.

The scholarship may be renewed in subsequent years dependent on performance. Awardees will be expected to become active members of the university sporting club for which the award has been granted.

While offering a comprehensive scholarship programme, TCD insists on students gaining entry by attaining the stated entry requirements. There are no entry points concessions.

Scholarships Provided Through the Department of Education and Skills (DES)

DEIS School Bursaries

In 2012, the then Minister for Education and Skills, Ruairi Quinn TD, established a scheme of bursaries for students from DEIS schools. Delivering Equality of Opportunity in Schools (DEIS) is a government initiative to address educational disadvantage. There are 849 schools in the programme.

- Bursaries will be awarded to the best-performing students based on their Leaving Certificate examination results.
- Awards will be made on a regional basis – Dublin, rest of Leinster, Munster, Connaught/Ulster.
- A minimum of sixty bursaries will be available in 2015.
- The amount of the bursary will be €2,000 per student per year of your course and will be paid as a single payment at the beginning of the academic year.
- Students to whom bursaries are awarded will also be entitled to apply for student grants towards the cost of maintenance and the student contribution or fees.

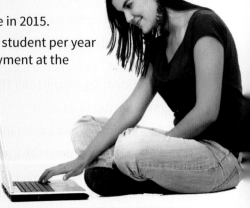

Qualifying criteria for the bursary is as follows:

✓ Attend a DEIS school.

✓ Be a first-time candidate for the Leaving Certificate.

✓ Be exempt from payment of the Leaving Certificate fee by virtue of holding a medical card.

✓ Take a third level course of at least two years' duration in a publicly-funded institution.

Bursaries will be paid annually for the duration of one undergraduate course and up to a maximum of four years postgraduate study. Applications are not necessary for these bursaries as they will be automatically awarded based on Leaving Certificate examination results.

Ernest Walton STEM Bursary (for Students from DEIS Schools)

As part of the Third Level Bursary Scheme, at least eight bursaries will be awarded on a regional basis (two each in Dublin, rest of Leinster, Munster, Connaught/Ulster) to students from DEIS schools who pursue courses at third level in the areas of Science, Technology, Engineering & Mathematics (STEM).

The bursary is named after Ernest Walton – Ireland's only Nobel laureate in science, and the man who, with John Cockcroft, became the first person to split the atom.

Qualifying criteria for the bursary is as follows:

- ✓ Attend a DEIS school.
- ✓ Be a first-time candidate for the Leaving Certificate.
- ✓ Be exempt from payment of the Leaving Certificate fee by virtue of holding a medical card.
- ✓ Have selected a STEM course as first choice on your CAO application.

The Ernest Walton STEM bursaries will be based both on Leaving Certificate results and on your course choice for third level so it will be necessary to make an application in order to be considered for the scheme.

- The amount of the bursary will be €2,000 per student per year of your course and will be paid as a single payment at the beginning of the academic year.
- Students to whom bursaries are awarded will also be entitled to apply for a student grant towards the cost of maintenance and the student contribution charge or fees.
- Bursaries will be paid annually for the duration of one undergraduate course and up to a maximum four years of postgraduate study.
- Each candidate must submit a completed application form and attach evidence from the CAO that he/she has applied for a STEM course as first choice.
- Third level courses of two or more years' duration, listed as STEM courses on the CareersPortal.ie website and pursued at a publicly-funded institution, will be considered.

The closing date for receipt of these applications is the end of July. They need to be submitted to: Higher Education – Equity of Access, Department of Education and Skills, Portlaoise Road, Tullamore, County Offaly.

All Ireland Scholarship Scheme

The All Ireland Scholarship Scheme is administered by the Department of Education & Skills and funded by businessman J. P. McManus.

This annual scholarship scheme provides third level education scholarships to 100 top performing Leaving Certificate students across the twenty-six counties who meet the eligibility criteria.

A minimum of two scholarships will be awarded each year to students from disadvantaged backgrounds in each county. The annual value of the scholarship is €6,750.

- ✓ No applications are necessary for the All Ireland Scholarships as they are awarded based on the Leaving Certificate exam results.

✓ They are available to first-time Leaving Certificate students who are exempt from paying the Leaving Certificate exam fee.

✓ Students must also have attended a non-fee paying post-primary school and participated in a Leaving Certificate programme there.

This scheme applies to the beneficiaries in Ireland only and a separate scheme applies for students resident in Northern Ireland. See www.allirelandscholarships.com for more information.

The Fund for Students with Disabilities

This fund provides grants for students who have serious sensory, physical, learning and/or communicative disabilities. The aim is to provide students with assistance and/or equipment to enable them to pursue and complete their course of study.

Applications for assistance are made by the Disability/Access Officer in the student's third level institution. The student, on registration for his/her course, should discuss his/her particular disability and the equipment or services required with the Disability/Access Officer. See www.studentfinance.ie for more information.

The Student Assistant Fund

This fund assists students who, having commenced a third level course, experience financial hardship and may be unable to continue their studies.

Applications for funding should be made by the individual student to the Access/Disability officer in their institution. The Student Assistance Fund is not available in further education/PLC colleges.

The fund is administered on a confidential, discretionary basis on behalf of the Minister for Education and Skills, by the Higher Education Authority. See www.studentfinance.ie for more information.